# Pasadena History Headline Quiz

690 Pasadena History Trivia Questions Taken from Pasadena Newspaper Headlines

by
Dan McLaughlin

**Pasadena History Headline Quiz:** 690 Pasadena history trivia questions taken from Pasadena newspaper headlines

Copyright © 2014 Dan McLaughlin

All rights reserved, including the right to reproduce this book or portions thereof in any form. For information contact **Dan McLaughlin, 469 E. Mountain Street, Pasadena CA 91104** or **pni.book@earthlink.net**.

All the images are all courtesy Pasadena Public Library through Pasadena Digital History Collaboration, Pasadena, California.

ISBN-13: 978-1492371502
ISBN-10: 1492371505
o (new pni)

*To Robin Weed-Brown the one who said,
"Make it happen."*

# Acknowledgments

Many people over the years have played a large part in producing the Pasadena News Index. Robin Weed-Brown was the supervisor who said, "Make it happen." Derek Massengale designed the search interface and has been the guardian all things ACCESS. Kim Myers made it work over the web and Pablo Olivia has shepherded though its recent iteration as an online entity.

Supervisors Carolyn Garner-Reagan; Darlene Bradley; Natasha Kahn; Christine Reeder; Martha Camacho and Janet Stone have found and fought for the resources to continue to make it happen.

Happy workers Jean Penn; Mark Cedeno; Rosa Casaretti; Siobhan Gambitto; Yvonne Hasegawa; Robert Bland; Nick Smith; Stephen Leeruangsri, Kevin Collins and Tara Smith have added their talent and expertise in actually doing the work. Some happy workers and contributors are known now only as initials: AA; am; and; CCP; CO; CV; CYR; EM; EO; evc; gmn; jb; JS; JV; lef; LL; ND; Sah; Sak; SE; sek; skg; SR; ST; SW;TJ; VF,

Three volunteers from the community, Daniel Weisman, Kathy Castro and Claralyn Howard have dedicated a measurable percentage of their life to adding content to the project.

Finally, Young Phong has taken "ownership" of the project in a truly impressive manner.

For this book Maura Weber proofread the manuscript, and Vendi Elmen was responsible for the layout. Vendi also was the guinea pig for many of the questions in their baby forms. Danica Dermott and her annual visit with her students from Walden School in Pasadena has prompted many of my ideas about the teaching of local history to students. The images are all courtesy Pasadena Public Library through the Pasadena Digital History Collaboration, Pasadena, California. Any mistakes in this book are mine alone.

Dan McLaughlin<br>
Pasadena, California<br>
February 2014

Hello Reader.

OK, you really DON'T have to read this part to understand or even enjoy this book.

You COULD just start randomly opening up pages and looking at the questions, and begin to test your knowledge of 690 fascinating tidbits about the history of Pasadena.

Or, you COULD go to the index and look for topics that are of interest, and start from there.

But go though all this stuff, you will get much much more out of it.

And I am betting that you are the intelligent, discerning, and yes, good-looking kind of person who wants to know the why behind the what.

So here are 690 questions about the history of Pasadena derived from the headlines of Pasadena newspapers, as displayed in the Pasadena Public Library's Pasadena News Index (PNI).

That means you should always mentally insert, "as reported by a Pasadena newspaper in the PNI," before each and every of the 690 questions that follow.

Actual reality may be different. If you happen to KNOW that the truth is something different, fine. But unless you can find a citation in the PNI that proves your point, for the purposes of this book, it doesn't matter.

Now if you have a newspaper clipping that has a date on it that proves your point, let us know at **pni.book@earthlink.net** and we will make some changes.

The miracle of self-publication on demand means that it's not that hard to change things.

This book is based part of a larger project to find innovative way to teach the history of Pasadena to grade-school children. I am a reference librarian at the Pasadena Public Library who has done local history for about 25 years, and I was asked by the children's department here at the library to put something together on the history of our fair city for when 4th graders come through doing their 4th grade local history assignment.

Since I wanted to make the process more interactive and show that history is figuring out how to answer questions that are of interest, I decided to sprinkle questions throughout the text of this yet unproduced tome to lure the reader into historical research. And I wanted questions that would require the reader to use the PNI to answer.

After plugging away for a bit, I soon realized that I had WAY too many questions to inflict on anyone in a narrative text setting, especially for a 4th grader, and so decided to spin off all the questions in another book.

This one. The one you are reading now.

Reflecting this pedagogical imperative, with each question there is a "help" which is basically a search string to find the citation in the PNI that provides the answer, and in many cases provides more information about the object of the question.

Each question has a larger story behind it: an 11-year-old boy who helped uncover an Indian burial ground in Pasadena; a Pasadena African-American who passed as white and served as an officer in World War One; a Pasadena woman who won a world chess championship.

To find out more about each answer you go to the PNI at **http://ww2.cityofpasadena.net/Library/PNI/subject.asp**. Then you follow the somewhat cryptic help attached to each question. (Basically the first phrase you type in as a subject search, then the next phrase is what you type in the search within a search box.)

**What is the PNI?**
Produced by the reference department at the Pasadena Public Library, the PNI is primarily an index that pulls out Pasadena-related items printed in local newspapers. Diligent library workers (also incredibly good-looking, by the way) read and then make citations to newspaper articles that deal with Pasadena in the *Pasadena Star-News*, *The Pasadena Journal*, the *Pasadena Weekly*, and occasional articles in the *Los Angeles Times*.

The results are made accessible through the Pasadena News index search portal **http://ww2.cityofpasadena.net/Library/PNI/subject.asp.**

We do not fully index any newspaper.

While by and large the content of the PNI only consists of citations (meaning you have to come to the library to actually read the article), there are links to online articles of the *Pasadena Weekly* from January 2006 to now.

Thank you, Kevin Uhrich.

Also if you have a library card, you can access full text articles online from the *Los Angeles Times* through the library's website **http://cityofpasadena.libguides.com/Databases**. Currently (2013) there are about 180,000 citations in the PNI. We try to be within 10 days of the current date when entering the main news pages of the *Pasadena Star-News*. Starting in June 1996, the PNI is the main source for Pasadena news citations. There are about 50,000 records from before that time, some of which are taken from already existing research files, others gathered in the course of conducting research on local history. These records cover (somewhat haphazardly) the time period with a slight emphasis on minority history, obituaries, and the Water and Power Department.

What follows is an extended discussion on how to search the PNI, and online searching in general.

Again, you don't need to continue, but if you wish to use your local history database to fully explore the main source of primary materials on Pasadena history, press on.

Still here?...Thank you...My, you ARE good-looking.

Basically, online searching is a process of winnowing the entire database into smaller components until you have only the parts that you need, without having discarded a relevant part along the way.

There are two basic ways to do this. One is to use a controlled vocabulary that groups like concepts together with a common term. For instance, all things Rose Parade, Rose Bowl Game, Rose Court, etc. are given the subject heading Tournament of Roses. In the PNI this type of search is the "subject search."

The other main way of searching is to search words that appear naturally in the information itself, much the way that Google searches the content of the documents that it delivers. In the PNI, we call this search the "phrase search." Use the phrase search if the search term is so unusual that it will lead you directly to the answer.

We also offer a third option, "author search," which searches the author field.

In general, I recommend using a subject search to get all the relevant articles, and then using a keyword search to narrow to the correct citation.

The structure of the PNI facilitates this search strategy.

In general, each question in this book should be answered within two search strings. There are no "trick" questions. The search terms that will lead to the answer are in the question. (There are some questions that have some math involved, though. For those you will have to use another source.)

In the PNI, search strings are automatically truncated at both ends of the search string. Truncation basically means whatever you type is the foundation for what the computer searches for. If the search string is truncated at both ends, a search string of the word **bat** will pull up the words **bat**s, **bat**tery, de**bat**ing, and acro**bat**s.

See how it works?

Boolean searching (refining your search with an additional information) is accomplished by using the "search within results" box that appears after the first search is executed. It is a Boolean "and" (further limiting) search. Subsequent searches in that box will only refer to the original search, not to the further reduced set.

For example, the search string *city council murder* will not pull up any article which the city council discussed murder, but rather would just look for the exact words city council murder in that order, which is a very unlikely phrase or subject heading.

If you wanted to actually do this search to find all the articles where the city council discussed murder, you should start with a subject search *city council* then in the "search within the search" box type *murder*.

In the PNI, capitalization does not matter, but spaces (which count as characters) do.

Because of this, less is more. Shorter search strings are more likely to get hits than longer elaborate search strings.

Citations are rendered in reverse chronological order.

Here is a discussion of the organizing principles of the PNI.

How many are still here?...My, so good-looking AND an inquiring mind. Very impressive.

With every newspaper article, in general, something (or someone) is doing something somewhere in Pasadena and each of those entry points can get assigned a subject heading. For instance, the city council can do city planning regarding the Old Town. In the article Bogaard, William J. could have responded to comments made by the Pasadena Chamber of Commerce.

And that is basically it.

We assign subject headings only that apply to Pasadena. That is to say we only add subject headings that describe the situation in Pasadena. If a Pasadenan is describing the gang situation in Glendale, for instance, we do not add a subject heading for Gangs. We add items of national or international importance only as they relate to Pasadena.

In general, we do not attempt to exhaustively provide access points to every possible entry point to an article. We assume that the patron will still have to scan a list of articles to get the most relevant to his/her needs.

We try and use Library of Congress Subject Headings and conventions whenever practical. Some of the more useful ones to link together like topics are:
*World War, 1914-1918*
*World War, 1939-1945*
*African Americans*

*Hispanic Americans*
*Women*

With the truncation feature mentioned above, the search string *1939-* is the same as typing out *World War, 1939-1945*

What follows is an even MORE exhaustive description of the cataloging conventions of the PNI.

Still here?...Your relatives are probably sick of hearing from your mom about how brilliant and perfect you have been ever since you were a baby and continuing to exist in that state of perfection to the present day...But it's good for them.

Basically if it's possible that an event may be written about in one year yet happens in another year we add a year component to the subject field. The examples are:
        A. *Rose Bowl, Year* (this refers only to the actual stadium, not the game.)
        B. *Tournament of Roses, Year*
        C. *Tournament of Roses, Year – Football Game, Floats, Theme, Grand Marshal, Queen and Princesses*
        D. *Elections, Year.* Combine with *City Council* (for City Council, formerly known as the Board of Directors), *School Management and Organization* (for School Board) or Mayor
        E. *Showcase House of Design, year*
        F. *Olympics, year*

Please note that with truncation, you can use this feature to limit your search to just the articles you want. For instance, a search string *Roses, 2012* will pull up all the articles about the 2012 Rose Parade, Game and Court. You could then do the search in the search in the search box football game or whatever. *Olympics, 193* will pull out all the articles about the 1932 and 1936 Olympics written at any time. You could then type in the name of sport you are interested in (*swimming, track and field, gymnastics*, etc.) to find all the articles about Pasadena swimmers in the 1932 or 1936 Olympics.

Articles about city departments or functions drop the word Pasadena in front of them. Thus it's just *Police Department; City Council; Commission on the Status of Women*, NOT Pasadena Police Department; Pasadena City Council; Pasadena Commission on the Status of Women. The only exception is the library, which goes with *Pasadena Public Library*. Hey, it's our database........And we're good-looking too.

We have some topics where we provide both a general subject heading and a more specific one.

The subject heading *Crime and Criminals* is applied to all articles involving any crime as well as the specific crime such as *Murder, Animal Welfare, Assault and*

*Battery, Automobile Theft, Demonstrations, Domestic Violence, Fraud, Gangs, Juvenile Delinquency, Kidnapping, Pornography, Prostitution, Rape, Sexual Assault, Embezzlement, Vandalism, Burglary, Robbery, Arson,* and *Child Abuse*. We also add the names of all the Pasadena people involved in the incident.

Any article about somebody suing someone else (civil actions) gets the subject heading *Actions and Defenses*. We do NOT index stories about trials that happen here in Pasadena if the crime in question did not happen in Pasadena, or involve residents of Pasadena.

For articles about the library, they all get the heading *Pasadena Public Library*, and if the event or news relates to a particular branch that branch name is also added (for instance *Central Library*, or *Allendale Branch Library*).

If an article mentions a city worker, they are also listed under their department *(City Manager, Fire Department)* AND under *Municipal Officials and Employees*.

For articles that deal with JPL, we are now adding the mission name as well. Thus we add mission names like *Galileo Spacecraft, Mars Program* and *Curiosity (Roving vehicles)* etc. to *Jet Propulsion Laboratory*. Note that entering the expression *Roving vehicles* will get all the citations dealing with cars on other planets.

*Schools* are added to any article dealing with an individual school. Schools named after people are entered under the full name of the person *John Muir High School; Francis E. Willard Elementary School*. If you want to pull up all the articles about a particular sports team of a school, do it in two steps. The name of the school *(Pasadena City College)*, followed by the name of the sport *(football, baseball,* etc.) will get you all the citations about PCC football, baseball etc.

We add the profession or occupational title ONLY if the person in question lives, works, or has some connection to Pasadena. Examples of this include *Authors, Artists, Musicians,* and *Physicians*. If the musician Yo-Yo Ma performs in Pasadena, we would add his name because be performed here, but would not add *Musician* because he does not live/work here. We add the occupational title to answer the question, "who are the 'artists' of Pasadena?"

We use *Visitors* for anyone of prominence who comes to Pasadena (like Yo-Yo Ma). We use *Royal Visitors* for visiting nobility and *Presidents – Journeys* for Presidents who have visited Pasadena before, during, or after their term of office. We also add the location in Pasadena that they visited.

We use *Charter* for anything about the organization of government and *Revenue* for anything about taxes or fees. *City Planning* covers anything about regulation of growth, housing or economic development in the city. *Water – Supply* will get you anything about the use of water and *Streets* will get you most things about streets, traffic and traffic engineering.

Other than the artful use of subject headings and phrases, there are several other ways the PNI allows you to limit the results of your search.

You can limit your search to only articles that link to the full text version of the article by clicking on the must link to full text version box. The other limit is the By Date filter. Below, this search would look for any article on Caltech (using a truncation of the official subject heading for Caltech, *California Institute of Technology*) from January 1, 1950 to December 31, 2010 that links to the full text of the article.

In the text of the book, the instruction to set dates to and from a certain date means using the by date feature seen above.

The other main useful filter is to limit the search by article type.

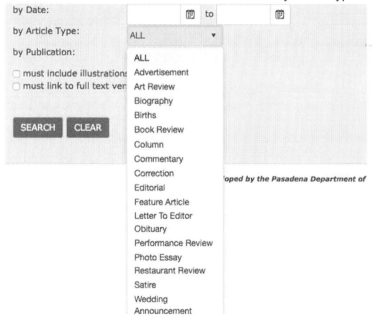

Let's go through all the article types. We're getting pretty close to the end. Consider this your bonus round.

The default article type is just a straight newspaper account of a contemporary event. There is no way to only get those articles. There is no separate identifier for these articles. These articles are the vast majority (66.3%) of the content of the PNI.

Advertisement: We occasionally index an advertisement when it is of a significant event or location. Currently about .75% of the content of the PNI is an advertisement.

Art review: A review of a Pasadena artist and/or of a show at a Pasadena art museum or gallery. this is a new category which we haven't used very much yet

Biography: A biographical article is one that basically offers a summary of a person's life or career not tied to a specific event. An article about a gentleman who loves cats over the course of his life would be a biographical article. The story of him adopting a specific cat would be a regular news article. Currently, about 1.5% of the PNI are biographical articles.

Births: These are news items announcing a birth. We do not index lists of births. Currently about .03% of the PNI are birth announcements.

Column: These are signed commentaries giving opinions by an individual printed on a regular basis. We do not fully index the output of any columnist, but only index content related to Pasadena. These articles can be useful to gauge popular reaction to the news. Currently about 3.1% of the PNI are columns.

Commentary: These are larger letters to the editor. They are signed, printed sporadically about Pasadena related issues. These articles can be useful to gauge popular reaction to the news. Currently about .6% of the PNI are commentaries.

Corrections: There are printed corrections or retractions. .04% of the PNI are corrections.

Editorial: These are unsigned opinions expressing the opinion of the newspaper on a topic. They can be useful summaries of how a particular issue was viewed by the community at a particular point in time. 1.6% of the PNI are editorials.

Feature article: A feature article is one that offers a summary or history of a particular topic not tied to a specific event. The story of wild animals interacting with humans would be a feature article. An article about a bear eating avocados in a back yard would be a regular news article. These articles are useful in revealing a broader treatment of an aspect of life in the community than a typical news article which is more closely tied to a specific event. Currently, 3.6% of the PNI are feature articles.

Letter to the editor: Shorter, signed sporadic commentaries, usually on a single topic. Can be useful to gauge public reaction to a topic, or depending on the author, informative of the viewpoint of an influential person. Currently, 6.1% of the PNI consists of letters to the editor.

Obituary: Items announcing someone's death. We index both paid (obituaries without headlines) and (obituaries with headlines) of anyone who lived, worked or went to school or church in Pasadena. Currently 10.8% of the PNI consists of obituaries.

Performance review: Generally we include the name of the play, location, and playwright. Anthony and Cleopatra by Shakespeare, William performed by A Noise Within is a good example. Bands are given the identifier (*Musical group*); movies (*Motion picture*); TV (*Television program*). These identifiers are also used when describing a movie or TV program filmed or otherwise connected with Pasadena. Currently performance reviews consists of .5% of the PNI.

Photo essays: These are articles that consist mostly of photos with a minimal amount of text. Currently 3.45% of the PNI are photo essays.

Restaurant review: An article that comments on the quality of food served at a restaurant. Currently 1.35% of the content of the PNI are restaurant reviews.

Satire: Lampoons, or spoofs of "real" news. Typically these are "April Fools" kind of articles. Only .01% of the PNI are satire.

Wedding announcements: Also includes accounts of weddings. Currently .2% of the PNI are wedding announcements.

Last, but not least, here is how we format street and personal names.

Still here? Simply amazing....You walk with the Gods, and look like them too.

Street names:
The general format for street addresses is name of street with the type of street spelled out, comma space direction space dash number. So 14 N. Fair Oaks Ave. would be

Fair Oaks Avenue, North – 14

If there is no direction, add the address directly after the comma. Thus 2222 Paloma Street would be

Paloma Street, 2222

Personal names:
The general convention is last name comma space first name space middle initial or name.

Smith, John

The space is important because it is counted as a character in the PNI.

Smith, John will return hits.
Smith,John will not. (Unless it's a typo)

Smith, would get all the people with the last name of Smith in the database.

In general we do not include honorifics such as Dr., Rev., and PhD. So Revered Allison Jones would be just

Jones, Allison

There are two exceptions, Mrs. when only the husband's name is used, and Jr. or Sr. or III.

We use the Mrs. when we need the Mrs. to distinguish between woman's name and her husband's. If there are some articles that use her first name and others that don't, we use her real first name as the subject and we include a SEE reference from the married name

Combs, Mrs. Theodore (only version we know.)
Prickett, Mrs. Charles F. SEE Prickett, Maudie
Prickett, Maudie

We use the Sr. and the Jr. to distinguish related people with the same name. When the person has a middle initial or name, use a comma following the middle name to separate it from the Jr. or the Sr.

Wyatt, Joseph Lucian, Jr.
Smith, Alton C., Sr.
Taylor, Joel E., III

Disclaimer: While these are the rules, we cannot guarantee that each and every record in the PNI conforms to each and every one of them. The process is done pretty much by hand, and while we are incredibly erudite, sophisticated, talented, and yes, good-looking, the simple fact is that errors do exist. If you find one (some) please let us know at pni.book@earthlink.net and we would be happy to make it better.

If you have any questions or comments about any of the questions, please contact me at pni.book@earthlink.net as well.

Thank you, and enjoy the book.

Dan McLaughlin
Pasadena, California

# Symbols Legend

| | | | |
|---|---|---|---|
| | Animals | | Holidays |
| | Arts & Entertainment | | Hotels |
| | Bridges | | Interesting Pasadenans |
| | Buildings | | Media |
| | Business & Economic Conditions | | Parks |
| | City of Pasadena | | Rose Bowl |
| | Children & Teens | | Schools |
| | Churches | | Sports |
| | Clubs & Groups | | Technology |
| | Crime and Criminals | | Thou Shalt Not |
| | Death & Health | | Tournament of Roses |
| | Disasters & Accidents | | Transportation |
| | Elections | | Visitors |
| | Ethnic Communities | | War |
| | Geography | | Women |

## Decades

| | | | | | | |
|---|---|---|---|---|---|---|
| **1880** | **1890** | **1900** | **1910** | **1920** | **1930** | **1940** |
| **1950** | **1960** | **1970** | **1980** | **1990** | **2000** | **2010** |

*Firefighters.*
*Three firemen putting out a small fire, maybe a training exercise?*

*ppl_13285*

1. The first driver of an electric automobile in Pasadena was a
    a. Man.
    b. Woman.

help: *electric automobiles* then scroll down to first one on the list


2. How many city employees potentially were eligible to enter the military draft for the Korean War?
    a. 2.
    b. 21.
    c. 221.
    d. 2,210.

help: *Korean War* then *and employees*


3. City Firefighter Erwin C. Draper would have been eligible to collect his pension in July 1940, but he died in February 1940 doing what?
    a. Driving too fast to get to a fire.
    b. Inhaling too much smoke.
    c. Playing in a football game against the police department.
    d. Turning off a water faucet.

**1940**

help: *Draper, Erwin c.*


4. When the Pasadena Fire Department played the Pasadena Police Department in a football game in 1930 in the Rose Bowl, eight players required medical attention. Only one player, however, suffered a concussion. Did that player, Patrolman McClanahan of the Police Department, play for the
    a. Losing team.
    b. Winning team.

help: *Rose Bowl, 1930* then *football*

5. Aside from suffering a concussion in a football game against the Fire Department in 1930, what else had Police Officer [in #4 he was called a Patrolman] McClanahan been commended for three years earlier?
   a. Shooting his pistol.
   b. Riding his motorcycle.
   c. Solving a murder.
   d. Writing poetry.

**1920**

help: limit by date to 1927 then *McClanahan*


6. The stated reason for the football contest between the Pasadena police and fire departments in 1930 in the Rose Bowl was to
   a. Claim bragging rights.
   b. Raise money for the unemployed.
   c. See which side had more fans in the city.
   d. Test the newly installed light system.

**1930**

help: *Rose Bowl, 1930* then *contest*


7. In 1929, the African American community submitted a petition to the City Council for its own
   a. Fire station.
   b. Hospital.
   c. Library.
   d. Police station.
   e. Park.

**1920**

help: limit by date to 1929, then *African americans* then *petition*

*Pasadena Police on patrol*    circa 1930    ppl_13155

8. Fumes caused by burning what affected a fireman in 1938?
   a. Drugs.
   b. Film.
   c. Oil.
   d. Shoes.

help: limit by date to 1938, then search by phrase *fireman*


9. In 1934, after being denied a pension by the city of Pasadena, Ida May Talbot, widow of city fireman Edgar Reece Talbot, requested his
   a. Badge.
   b. Heart.
   c. Horse.
   d. Uniform.

help: *Talbot, Ida May*


10. California Institute of Technology, along with MIT, sponsored a "smogless" auto race (featuring electric automobiles) in
   a. 1950.
   b. 1970.
   c. 1990.
   d. 2010.

help: search by phrase *smogless*


11. There have been electric automobiles on Pasadena streets since
   a. 1898.
   b. 1908.
   c. 1978.
   d. 2008.

help: *electric automobiles* then scroll down to first one on the list

12. How many times have there been accidents involving horses and electric automobiles?
   a. None.
   b. One.
   c. Two.
   d. Five.

Pasadena Ice Company          ppl_220

help: *electric automobiles* then *horses*


13. Inflation strained the patience of housewives in what year?
   a. 1919.
   b. 1946.
   c. 1966.
   d. 1974.

help: *inflation* then *housewives*


14. The first driver of an electric vehicle involved in an accident was a
   a. Man.
   b. Woman.

help: *electric automobiles* then *accidents* scroll down to first one on the list


15. In the 1940's, radio waves for radio station DBNY (heard in a dorm at California Institute of Technology) were transmitted through the
   a. Air.
   b. Plumbing.
   c. Radiator.
   d. Telephone.

help: *DBNY (Radio station)*

16. In 1952, Diane Dunbar sent to John Klotzle, a GI serving in Korea, a 131-foot long what?
   a. Letter.
   b. Sandwich.
   c. Scarf.
   d. Paper chain.

**1950**

help: *Dunbar, Diane*


17. The Korean War ended in 1953. Fifty-one years later Richard R. Hines Jr. got what from it?
   a. An apology delayed by stubborness
   b. A letter delayed in the mail.
   c. A medal delayed in the bureaucracy.
   d. A promotion delayed by his race.

**1950**

help: *Hines, Richard*


18. Many Pasadenans have served in two wars. Using information from obituaries, which two wars have people from Pasadena served in the most?
   a. The Spanish American War and World War One.
   b. World War One and World War Two.
   c. World War Two and the Korean War.
   d. The Korean War and the Vietnamese War.

help: Limit by type to obituary, then *Spanish-American War,* then *1914-1918.* Note number of citations. Keeping article type set to obituary, do a new search with *World War, 1914-1918* then *1939-1945*: *World War, 1939-1945* and *Korean war*; *Korean War* and *Vietnamese conflict*

*Civil War Memorial*
*Sculpture entitled "Volunteer of '61' dedicated May 13, 1906. Designed by Theo Alice Ruggles-Kittson in Memorial Park.*

ppl_3659

19. What is the last name of a Nobel Prize winner in physics who was also seen frequently painting along the Arroyo Seco in the 1920's?
answer: _____

**1920**

help: *Arroyo Seco* then *physics* (or *Nobel Prize*)


20. Robert Lang, a California Institute of Technology graduate, combines the study of physics with the art of:
   a. Ceramics.
   b. Kinetic sculpture.
   c. Kite design and flying.
   d. Origami.

help: *Lang, Robert*


21. The Nobel Prize winner who visited Pasadena in 1916 won the Nobel Prize for:
   a. Chemistry.
   b. Literature.
   c. Medicine.
   d. Physics.

**1910**

help: Limit by date to any in 1916, then *Nobel Prize*


22. The Nobel Prize winner who visited Pasadena in 1916 came from:
   a. England.
   b. Germany.
   c. India.
   d. Sweden.

**1910**

help: Limit by date to any in 1916, then *Nobel Prize*.

23. In 1918, what was the new course taught at Throop Polytechnic Institute because of America's entry into World War One?
   a. Airplane design.
   b. Bridge building.
   c. Bridge demolition.
   d. Ship construction.

help: Limit by date to 1918, then *Throop Poly* then *new course*


24. When military instruction was made part of Throop's curriculum before the United States joined World War One, what class was part of the training course?
   a. Airplane design.
   b. Bridge building.
   c. Food engineering.
   d. Ship construction.

help: *Throop Poly* then *military instruction*


25. People associated with California Institute of Technology have died in accidents everywhere EXCEPT:
   a. An astronomy lab.
   b. A football field.
   c. A radiation lab.
   d. A swimming pool.

help: Limit by article type to obituary, then *of technology* then *accidents*

*Bridge building, Throop College. Scan from the article "Gate Ways to Pasadena" written by John J. Hamilton, Commissioner of Public Parks and Buildings, in California Southland, School Number issue (August / September) 1919, pg. 15.*

ppl_10696

26. In 1946, what almost killed Caltech student William Jacobs?
    a. Boxing.
    b. Football.
    c. Skiing.
    d. Sky-diving.

**1940**

help: *Jacobs, William*


27. What had been removed from food engineered at California Institute of Technology that was sent to France to feed tubercular children in 1945?
    a. Salt.
    b. Sugar
    c. Water.
    d. Wine.

**1940**

help: limit by dates to 1945, then *of technology* then *France*


28. It cost $100,000 in 1947. Caltech was quite proud of its mechanical what?
    a. Brain.
    b. Kidney.
    c. Lung.
    d. Hand.

**1940**

help: *of technology* then *mechanical*


29. Franklin Thomas was both a California Institute of Technology professor and a member of the City Council. How many of his sons served in the military during World War Two, which lasted from 1939-1945?
    a. None.
    b. One.
    c. Two.
    d. Five.

**1940**

help: *Thomas, Franklin* then *World War, 1939*

30. In 1942, California Institute of Technology professor Henry Borsook used students to test his ideas on
   a. Diet.
   b. Exercise.
   c. Radiation.
   d. Psychology.

**1940**

help: *Borsook,* then *students*


31. The Unidentified Flying Object (UFO) sighted above Oak Grove Park in 1956 was really a California Institute of Technology
   a. Balloon.
   b. Helicopter.
   c. Prank.
   d. Rocket test.

**1950**

help: *of technology* then *Oak Grove Park*


32. The Unidentified Flying Object (UFO) sighted above Pasadena in 1966 was really a California Institute of Technology
   a. Balloon.
   b. Helicopter.
   c. Prank.
   d. A and C.
   e. B and C.

**1960**

help: *of technology* then *flying objects*

*Main Entrance Throop Insitute.*
*Caltech was founded in 1891 under the name of Throop University. In 1892 the school was renamed Throop Polytechnic Institute, and in 1913 Throop Institute of Technology. In 1920 the current name of California Institute of Technology was applied to the school.*
*1905*

ppl_7075

33. In 1968 which presidential candidate spent the day in Pasadena?
   a. Eugene McCarthy.
   b. George McGovern.
   c. Hubert Humphrey.
   d. Richard Nixon.
   e. Robert F. Kennedy.

**1960**

help: *elections, 1968* then *spent the day*


34. What is the last name of the Pasadena resident most closely connected to Robert F. Kennedy?
Answer: _____

**1960** ★

help: *Kennedy, Robert F.*


35. What city's temple did Raphael Goldenstein serve in before being the first rabbi at Temple B'nai Israel in 1923?
   a. Albuquerque.
   b. Chicago.
   c. New York.
   d. Stockton.

**1920**

help: *Goldenstein, Ra*


36. What high school did RFK assassin Sirhan Bishara Sirhan go to?
   a. Blair.
   b. John Marshall.
   c. John Muir.
   d. Pasadena.

**1960**

help: *sirhan, sirhan* then *high school*

37. What were two of the last names of the Pasadenans who died in 9/11? (hint: there are four last names for five people)

Answers: _____, _____

**2000**

help: Limit by article type to obituary, then *World Trade Center*


38. What were 114,000 of needed in April 1942?
   a. Dollars to fully subscribe to the First Victory Loan.
   b. Pounds of scrap metal to fulfill the quota.
   c. Sugar ration cards to legally buy sugar.
   d. Travel vouchers for Japanese being sent to Manzanar.

**1940**

help: Search by phase *114,000*


39. In December 2001, N. Y. firefighters did what to get to Pasadena?
   a. Bicycled.
   b. Hitchhiked.
   c. Skipped.
   d. Walked.

**2000**

help: Search by phrase *N. Y. firefighters*


40. Richard Ustick, a military cook during the Korean War, didn't worry about what in his beans?
   a. Bacon.
   b. Bullets.
   c. Ballast.
   d. Bridge work.

**1950**

help: *Ustick*

41. Russell J. Brown from Pasadena was the first what of the Korean War?
   a. One in a uniform to get shot by a Korean.
   b. One in a suit get a "Welcome Back to the Army" letter.
   c. One in a uniform to fire an artillery shell at a Korean.
   d. One in a jet shoot down another jet.

**1950**

help: *Brown, Russell*


42. What did NOT close down in the immediate aftermath of 9/11?
   a. Caltech.
   b. City Hall.
   c. JPL.

**2000**

help: *World trade Center* then *close*


43. What Pasadena street has been suggested as a place for a memorial for 9/11? (Spell out all the words.)
Answer: _____

help: *World trade center* then *memorials*


44. The *Pasadena Weekly* said in 2007, the best place to hear hip-hop was the
   a. 35er.
   b. Colorado.
   c. Lucky Baldwin's.
   d. Club Menage.

**2000**

help: Limit by dates from 2007, then *hip-hop* then *best place to hear*

*Along the Colorade Street Bridge*
*This photo was between 1913, construction of the Colorado Street Bridge, and 1920, construction of the of the central tower of the Vista Del Arroyo Hotel building (the series of buildings on the other side of the bend in the bridge).*

*ppl_26*

45. The musical group Crown City Rockers played what kind of music?
   a. Classic Rock.
   b. Hip-hop.
   c. Metal.
   d. Rockabilly.

help: *Crown City Rockers (Musical group)*


46. In current (2013) dollars, about how much was the cost of constructing an annex to the library in 1900?
   a. $2,820.
   b. $28,200.
   c. $282,000.
   d. $2,820,000.

**1900**

help: Limit by date to 1900, then *Central Library* then *annex* Then go to Google and type *current value of a dollar*. Go to a website like measuring worth.com/uscompare and make the calculation.


47. Which national association was going to meet in Pasadena in 1911?
   a. American Library Association.
   b. National American Woman's Suffrage Association.
   c. National Squash Tennis Association.
   d. Playground Association of America.

**1910**

help: Limit by date to 1911, then *association* then *meet*


48. Which city department probably cared the most when a national association met in Pasadena in 1911?
a. City Attorney.
b. Fire.
c. Library.
e. Police.

**1910**

help: Limit by date to 1911, then *association* then *meet*

49. California Governor Hiram Warren Johnson visited Pasadena in 1911 to
   a. Give a commencement address.
   b. Look for votes.
   c. Talk to librarians.
   d. Vacation.

**1910**

help: Limit by date to 1911 then *Johnson, hiram*


50. In an attempt to guard the collection in 1911, Library Trustees did what?
   a. Bought a safe.
   b. Hired a guard.
   d. Publicly named people with overdue books.
   c. Raised overdue fines.

**1900**

help: Search by phrase *guard collection*


51. In 1910, new steel stacks at the library cost less than what in 2013 dollars (about)?
   a. $1,250.
   b. $12,500.
   c. $125,000.
   d. $1,250,000.

**1910**

help: Search by phrase *new steel stacks* Then go to Google and type *current value of a dollar*. Go to a website like measuring worth.com/uscompare and make the calculation.


52. When Al Gore visited Pasadena in 2013, he said something had been hacked. Was it
   a. Complancency.
   b. Democracy.
   c. Science.
   d. Trust.

**2010**

help: limit by date to 2013, then *Gore, Al*

53. James A. Garfield Elementary School had classes in what in its curriculum in 1921?
Answer:_____

**1920**

help: *James A. Garfield* then *curriculum*


54. Which Pasadena school made a floral design for a visiting president?
    a. Columbia Grammar School.
    b. James A. Garfield Elementary.
    c. James Madison Elementary School.
    d. Lincoln Avenue School.

help: *president* then *floral design*


55. Students at which Pasadena school were especially sad when President Harding did not visit them in 1923?
    a. Abraham Lincoln Elementary School.
    b. Andrew Jackson Elementary School.
    c. George Washington Elementary School.
    e. James Madison Elementary School.

**1920**

help: Limit by date to 1923, then *Harding* then *school*


56. In 1927, Gordon Hawkins, an African American football hero at Pasadena Junior College, died when his car was hit by a
    a. Car.
    b. Deer.
    c. Lamppost.
    d. Train.

**1920**

help: *Hawkins, Gordon*

57. In July, 1924, even before the school was announced it was accepting students, how many people had applied to Pasadena Junior College?
   a. 5.
   b. 15.
   c. 50.
   d. 150.

**1920**

help: Limit by date from July 1, 1924 to July 31, 1924, then *junior college*


58. Because of a technicality, Pasadena Junior College started in 1924 as a
a. High school.
b. Night school.
c. Segregated school.
d. Single-sex school.

**1920**

help: Limit by date to 1924, then *junior College* then *technicality*


59. Manuel Rustin, of John Muir High School, won the Milken award in 2012. The Milken is considered the "Oscar" of what?
   a. Painting.
   b. Student filmmaking.
   c. Teaching.
   d. Thinking.

**2010**

help: *Rustin, M*


60. In the 2012 presidential campaign, who was the only Republican candidate who came to Pasadena for a second visit?
   a. Herman Cain.
   b. Newt Gingrich.
   c. Michele Bachmann.
   d. Rick Perry.

**2010**

help: *elections, 2012* then *second*

61. Just before Chinese New Year in 1911, the arrival of what caused a rush at the bargain counter?
   a. Brooms.
   b. Firecrackers.
   c. Red envelopes.
   d. Turtles.

help: *Chinese New Year* then *bargain counter*


62. In 2012, John Johnson of California Institute of Technology discovered three new
   a. Fish
   b. Elements
   c. Minerals
   d. Planets

help: *johnson, john* then *three new*


63. The "Devil Inside" (the motion picture, not the archfiend) used what Pasadena location in its advertising?
   a. Kidspace.
   b. La Pintoresca Branch Library.
   c. Pasadena City Hall.
   d. Westminster Presbyterian Church.

help: *Devil Inside*


64. In 1909, firecrackers celebrating Chinese New Year kept the city awake for:
   a. 10 minutes.
   b. 1 hour.
   c. 10 hours.
   d. 1 day.

help: *Chinese New Year* then *awake*

65. (Complete the phrase) Often seen performing at the annual party hosted by Pasadena Heritage on the Colorado Street Bridge is the musical group Snotty Scotty and the _____?
   a. Antihistamines.
   b. Cough Syrups.
   c. Expectorants.
   d. Hankies.

help: *snotty scotty and*

Arroyo Seco and the Colorado Bridge     ppl_24

66. When 90's favorite Sugar Ray showed up for a concert at the Rose Bowl in 2012, what was NOT notable about the show?
   a. He showed up.
   b. It was free.
   c. The people of Linda Vista were happy to see him.
   d. There was running involved.

**2010**

help: *Sugar Ray*

67. In 2012, the Beautiful Mind of John Nash was on display, live at
   a. California Institute of Technology.
   b. Fuller Theological Seminary.
   c. Pasadena Civic Auditorium.
   d. Pasadena Pubic Library.

**2010**

help: *nash, John*

68. When W. H. Connelly paid a $25 "Booze Fine" in 1925, technically he was
   a. 'Dead'.
   b. 'Drunk'.
   c. 'Guilty as sin'.
   d. 'Not himself'.

**1920**

help: *Connelly, w.*


69. The Pasadena Patriots have been a football team (1964); a drill team (1984), and a more recently a
   a. Cooking group.
   b. Historical reenacting group.
   c. Musical group.
   d. Political group.

help: *Pasadena Patriots*


70. In 2012, the big Nowruz (Iranian New Year) party was held at
   a. Neighborhood Church.
   b. Noor Restaurant Ballroom.
   c. Pasadena Elks Lodge.
   d. Scottish Rite Temple.

**2010**

help: Search by phrase *nowruz*


71. In 1982 Saint Andrew's Church sued the City of Pasadena over what?
   a. Poor trash pick-up.
   b. Their contract with Planned Parenthood.
   c. Rowdy parties on Raymond.
   d. Uneven application of zoning rules.

*Track removal North of Walnut, 10-28-40 Raymond Avenue. Saint Andrews Church is the church tower in the background*
*ppl_3366*

**1980**

help: *Saint Andrew* then *sued*

72. In 1957, 1000 mothers marched on
   a. Cancer
   b. Diabetes
   c. Heart disease
   d. Polio

**1950**

help: Search by phrase *1000 mothers*


73. Queen Noor visited Pasadena in 2001. She was Queen of
   a. Jordan.
   b. Thailand.
   c. The Netherlands.
   d. Swaziland.

**2000**

help: *Noor,*


74. President Thai is a
   a. Cruise ship.
   b. Dog.
   c. Restaurant.
   d. Superhero.

help: *President thai*


75. Francisco Javier Mora was murdered at California Institute of Technology in 1995. Raul Romero was arrested for the crime in
   a. 1995.
   b. 1997.
   c. 2002.
   d. 2010.

**1990**

help: *Romero, Raul* then *arrested*

76. Pasadena resident Gale Anne Hurd owns a Pasadena restaurant, Vertical Wine Bistro, which serves dead food to live people, and produces a TV show which shows dead creatures who feed off live people. The show is
    a. Buffy the Vampire Slayer.
    b. Dead Set.
    c. Walking Dead.
    d. Zombie Beer Run.

help: *Hurd, Gale anne* then *television*


77. "Play Me, I'm Yours'" was a public art piece in 2012 involving
    a. Batting cages.
    b. Etch-a-Sketches.
    c. Pianos.
    d. Video poker.

help: Search by phrase *Play me, i*


78. On May 21, 1969, Pasadena's anti-war vigil regarding the Vietnamese War went into its _____ year?
    a. First.
    b. Second.
    c. Third.
    d. Fourth.
    e. Fifth.

**1960**

help: Limit date to and from 05/21/1969. Leave the box you type in empty, hit search.


79. What is the first name of the Pasadena resident most closely connected to Robert F. Kennedy?
Answer: _____

**1960**

help: *Kennedy, Robert F.*

*A Gallery at the "Baby Hole" (1925) at the The Pasadena Golf Club which is now known as the Altadena Town and Country Club.*                    *ppl_6046*

80. In 2012, the Pasadena Jewish Temple celebrated its _____ anniversary?
   a. 50th.
   b. 70th.
   c. 90th.
   d. 110th.

**2010**

help: *Pasadena jewish* then *anniversaries*


81. In 1925, California Institute of Technology announced that its new Seismological Institute was to be built next to which golf course in Pasadena?
   a. Annandale.
   b. Carmelita.
   c. Brookside.
   d. Eaton Canyon.

**1920**

Help: Limit by date to 1925, then *California instit* then *golf*

82. In 1940, Anna J. Hammer was found hanging dead in a hotel room closet. In the room was soon to be former Pasadena Police Officer Frank Alexander. The coroner at her inquest ruled that she was "probably
   a. Angry."
   b. Drunk."
   c. Insane."
   d. Suicidal."

**1940**

help: *Hammer, Anna* then *probably*


83. In 1930 the Fourth of July at the Rose Bowl had a last minute attraction, the Pride of Missouri. The "Pride" was a
   a. Firework display.
   b. House made of corncobs.
   c. Mule.
   d. State beauty queen.

**1930**

help: *Rose Bowl, 1930* then *Missouri*


84. "Lucky Tuffy" was a what from Pasadena?
   a. An agile dog who delighted in chasing horses.
   b. A skinny wrestler whose motto was "Better Lucky than Good."
   c. A prominent football player whose name was used for a tungsten mine.
   d. A near-sighted pilot who walked away from many landings in better shape than his planes.

help: Search by phrase *Lucky Tuffy*

*This is the float "Shape of Things to Come" done by the City of South Pasadena for the 1954 Rose Parade.*
*ppl_h2421*

85. Which Rose Parade had the first woman named to judge the floats?
    a. 1922.
    b. 1942.
    c. 1962.
    d. 1982.
    e. 2002.

help: *Floats* then *first woman*


86. In the 1953 World Series there were three Pasadenans: Jackie Robinson, Dick Williams and
    a. Darrell Evans.
    b. Irv Noren.
    c. Loren Ury.
    d. Stan Gray.

**1950**

help: Search by phrase *World Series* then *three*


87. On Swinging Saturday in May, 2011
    a. A playground (for kids of all abilities) opened in Brookside Park.
    b. Charles Fuller (a monkey) escaped in the trees on Orange Grove.
    c. Jonathan Stout and His Campus Five (a musical group) performed at Grace Hall.
    d. A "wild orgy" (complete with dancing girls and booze) began in the Arroyo Seco.

**2010**

help: Search by phase *Swinging saturday*

*#2 10 ton steam roller Jan. 1938*
*ppl_3337*

88. In 1988 to celebrate Israel's 50th birthday, students at Chaim Weizmann School created a
  a. Map.
  b. Model kibbutz.
  c. Mosaic.
  d. Musical play.

**1980**

help: *Chaim weiz* then *50th birthday*


89. Two members of the United States Supreme Court have been Grand Marshals of the Rose Parade; Earl Warren in 1955 and _____ in 2006.
  a. Anton Scalia.
  b. Ruth Bader Ginsberg.
  c. Sandra Day O'Connor.
  d. William Rehnquist.

**2000**

help: *of roses, 2006* then *Supreme Court*


90. In 1919 Gurlay Dunn-Webb, a Pasadenan, was the only woman pro what?
  a. Golfer.
  b. Polo player.
  c. Swimmer.
  d. Tennis player.

**1910**

Help: *Dunn-webb*


91. Dick Williams had to wait how many years before being accepted into Baseball's Hall of Fame in 2008?
  a. 5.
  b. 10.
  c. 15.
  d. 20.

**2000**

help: *Williams, Dick* then *Hall of Fame*

92. Albert Ching, owner of the White Hut Restaurant, was also a famous
   a. Magician.
   b. Marine biologist.
   c. Math teacher.
   d. Musician.

help: *Ching, Albert*


93. Perhaps annoyed by the amount he usually tipped, in 1926 A. K. Bourne got a letter saying he would be killed unless he paid $1,000 to Rey Bergman and M. A Selementi. These men were employees of the Annandale Golf Club. They were employed as
   a. Caddies.
   b. Car valets.
   c. Groundskeepers.
   d. Waiters.

help: *Bourne, A. K.* then *bergman*


94. In 2013, the Gold Line celebrated its _____ birthday
a. 5th.
b. 10th.
c. 15th.
d. 20th.

**2010**

help: Search by phrase *Gold Line* then *birthday*


95. In 2013, Geoffrey Blake of California Institute of Technology saw what in space?
   a. Rocks.
   b. Reindeer.
   c. Snow.
   d. Trash.

help: *Blake, Geoffrey*

96. Who is the United States Supreme Court Justice who visited Pasadena in 2013?
    a. Anthony Kennedy.
    b. Clarence Thomas.
    c. Sonia Sotomayor.
    d. Stephen Breyer.

**2010**

help: Limit by date to 2013, then *United States. Supreme* then *visitors*


97. Golf great Walter Hagen played at which golf course in 1926?
    a. Annandale.
    b. Brookside.
    c. Midwick.
    d. Pasadena Country Club.

**1920**

help: *Hagen, Walter*


98. I fly through the air 'cause I can,
    I fight pirates before I'm a man.
    My outline is complete,
    And made of concrete,
    In a room named after me, Peter Pan.
    Where am I?
Answer: _____ (Two words.)

help: Search by phrase *Peter Pan* then *room*


99. Sam Han helps orphans from
    a. China.
    b. North Korea.
    c. Singapore.
    d. Thailand.

help: *Han, sam* then *orphans*

*Breaking ground at the Pasadena Civic Auditorium. Men standing around steam shovel. This view is looking towards the north. The dome is Pasadena City Hall.*

*ppl_109*

100. Perhaps as a Christmas gesture, in December 2011 the city announced that its expensive and unenforceable program would be ending in June of 2012. The program involved
    a. Fences.
    b. Dogs.
    c. Parking.
    d. Cameras.

**2010**

help: Limit by date to December 2011 then search by phrase *expensive*


101. New Horizon School opened in 1999 and received top U. S. honors in 2005. What religious tradition is it in?
    a. Buddhism.
    b. Christianity.
    c. Islam.
    d. Judaism.

**1990 2000**

help: *New Horizon* then *top honors*

102. In 1989 which school had the most Merit Scholars?
   a. John Muir.
   b. La Salle.
   c. Pasadena Poly.
   d. Westridge.

**1980**

help: Limit by date to 1989 then *school* then *merit scholars*


103. The Olympic Team tryouts for which sport were held in Pasadena in 1920?
   a. Bicycling.
   b. Diving.
   c. Soccer.
   d. Track and field.

**1920**

help: *Olympics, 1920* then *tryouts*


104. As reported in the *Pasadena Star-News*, how many veterans of World War One tried to or committed suicide?
   a. 0.
   b. 3.
   c. 6.
   d. 9.

help: Limit by publication to *Pasadena Star-News*, then *1914-1918* then *suicide*

105. When was the first time that the phrase "higher tuition" was used in connection with California Institute of Technology?
   a. 1920.
   b. 1970.
   c. 1990.
   d. 2010.

help: *California Inst* then *higher tuition*

106. PCC did what to honor Douglas Yuki, who died in Vietnam in 1971?
   a. Built a monument.
   b. Dedicated a classroom.
   c. Established a scholarship.
   d. Planted some trees.

**1970**

help: *Yuki, Douglas*


107. Starting in 2012, members of what community have wanted a memorial to their genocide in a Pasadena park?
   a. African American.
   b. Armenian.
   c. Jewish.
   d. Hispanic American.

**2010**

help: Limit by date from date of 01/01/2012, then *memorial*, then *genocide*


108. After Floyd Gerald Thayer came back from the Spanish American War (1898) and got a job, the expression that would mostly likely have been on his business card was
   a. Floyd Gerald Thayer, Esq.
   b. Floyd Thayer, DDS.
   c. Floyd the Magnificent.
   d. Officer F. G. Thayer.

**1890**

help: *Thayer, Floyd Gerald*

109. John Charles England, who had attended Pasadena Junior College was a war hero during World War Two. For that he had something named after him that received a presidential citation for outstanding job in combat during the war. The thing was
    a. An airplane.
    b. A rocket.
    c. A ship.
    d. A tank.

**1940**

help: *England, John*


110. Pasadena resident Charles Johnson was the first African-American employed as what on the Southern Pacific Railroad?
    a. Conductor.
    b. Dining car steward.
    c. Engineer.
    d. Station agent.

help: *Johnson, Charles* then *Southern Pacific*


111. Margaret White would have successfully jumped off the Colorado Street Bridge and killed herself in 1930 EXCEPT
    a. A fireman lunged and caught her when she jumped.
    b. It had just rained and there was too much water in the Arroyo below.
    c. She did not look before she jumped and only fell 25 feet.
    d. The portable trampoline held by policemen actually worked.

**1930**

help: *White, margaret*

112. The first anti-tobacco (or cigarettes) campaign in Pasadena was in
   a. 1906.
   b. 1931.
   c. 1966.
   d. 1991.

help: Limit by date to end in 1991, then *cigarettes* then scroll down to the bottom

113. In 1946, Oliver M. Haney, a veteran of the Civil War, said he had given up what 87-year habit to keep in condition to vote?
   a. Beer.
   b. Beef.
   c. Cigars.
   d. Sugar.

help: Limit by date to 1946, then *Haney, Oliver*

114. Which city department's main building has a piece of art by "the Godfather of California Light and Space"?
   a. Fire.
   b. Library.
   c. Police.
   d. Public Works.

help: Search by phrase *godfather of California*

115. (Fill in the blank.) In 1974, the *Pasadena Star-News* had a headline, "Next 100 years: Perils of New _____"
    a. Affluence."
    b. Economy."
    c. Poverty."
    d. Technology."

**1970**

help: Search by phrase *Perils of new*


116. Paul Rogers is an artist who brings Santa to life in
    a. Balloons.
    b. Murals.
    c. Person.
    d. Stamps.

help: *Rogers, Paul*


117. In 2000, which award ceremony attracted the attention of the Pasadena Police Department at the Pasadena Civic Auditorium?
    a. Emmy Awards.
    b. People's Choice Awards.
    c. Soul Train Lady of Soul Awards.
    d. Source Hip-Hop Music Awards.

**2000**

help: Limit by date to 2000, then *police department* then *awards*


118. When was the first time someone complained about the poor lighting at the Central Library?
    a. 1907.
    b. 1927.
    c. 1941.
    d. 1989.

help: *Central library* then *light* then scroll down to the bottom of the list

119. When was the first recorded protest over the city's parking plan for Colorado Boulevard made to the city council?
   a. 1898.
   b. 1906.
   c. 1921.
   d. 1928.

help: *Colorado Boulevard* then *parking plan*


120. BotCon, held at the Pasadena Center annually from 2004 to 2011, was a celebration of all things
   a. Anime.
   b. Batman.
   b. Bottle Caps.
   d. Transformers.

help: *Botcon*


121. When teens Jay Page and Melvill Humble jumped off the Colorado Street Bridge in 1928, they had a plan. As far as they had thought it through, the plan was
   a. Catch a branch of a nearby tree.
   b. Hit the water; avoid the rocks.
   c. Hope that their homemade hang glider would work well enough.
   d. Wish that the other guy would chicken out first.

**1920**

help: *Page, Jay*


122. In 1916, "vacation rules" at the Pasadena Public Library meant
   a. Librarians wore Hawaiian shirts.
   b. Little umbrellas were placed in the books.
   c. Patrons could check out more books for longer periods of time.
   d. The no shoes/no service policy was not enforced.

**1910**

help: *vacation rules*

123. Tourists got what for free from the city in 1911 in Pasadena?
   a. Basket of oranges.
   b. Bus tokens
   c. Library use.
   d. Map of the city.

**1910**

help: Limit by date to 1911, then search by phrase *tourists*


124. I once took a clipper to go fro and to in,
   My testimony to Ickes was a ruin.
   I studied oil in war,
   And I did so much more,
   And my pavilion on campus is a Bruin.
What is my last name?
Answer: _____

help: Search by phrase *Ickes* then either *testimony* or *clipper*


125. What Pasadena location was mined for gold in 1914?
   a. Brookside Park.
   b. Eaton Canyon.
   c. Maryland Hotel.
   d. Mount Wilson.

**1910**

help: Search by phrase *mined for gold*


126. In 1914, why did Charles Grimes want Tom Reed to get plenty of cyanide?
   a. He didn't like him very much.
   b. He really believed it would help his toothache.
   c. He thought it would make Tom work better.
   d. Mrs. Reed told him to do it.

**1910**

help: *Tom Reed* then *cyanide*

127. In 1928, Pasadenans consumed 10,600 gallons of this a day (it worked out to about a pint a day)
   a. Gin.
   b. Milk.
   c. Water.
   d. Wine.

**1920**

help: Search by phrase *10,600*

128. USC and Caltech have played football against each other at least twice. USC has always been USC and Caltech once in 1896 played as Throop Polytechnic Institute and once in 1927 as California Institute of Technology. Which of the following is true
   a. Both times Throop/Caltech scored 0 points.
   b. Both times USC scored 0 points.
   c. Each school scored 0 points once.

**1890 1920**

help: Limit by date to 1896, then *Throop* then *football*. Then reset limit by date to 1927. Then *of technology* then *football*

129. The annual Turkey Tussle is a
   a. Dinner given to people every Thanksgiving weekend in Central Park.
   b. Car show dedicated to the Ford Pinto on Green Street.
   c. Football game between John Muir High School and Pasadena High School in the Rose Bowl.
   d. Pet show sponsored by the Pasadena Humane Society.

help: *Turkey Tussle*

*Goal in Tournament Park football grounds. Consul the trained monkey, Marie's pet.*
*This seems to be a series of photos taken to document a fair put on by the Pasadena Elks Lodge in Tournament Park, California in 1923.*

*ppl_6008f*

130. The first major league team to win a baseball game in Pasadena played at Tournament Park in 1909. That team was the
   a. Boston Americans.
   b. Chicago Cubs.
   c. Chicago White Sox.
   d. Pittsburgh Pirates.

**1900**

help: Limit by date to 1909, then *baseball team* then *Tournament Park*


131. According to a *Pasadena Star-News* article written in 1937, in 1936 careless smokers cost the county about (in 2013 dollars) to fight fires
   a. $150,000.
   b. $1,110,000.
   c. $5,900,000.
   d. $11,100,000

**1930**

help: Search by phrase *careless smokers* then Google current value of a dollar, then convert at a web site like measuringworth.com/uscompare


132. Pasadena received national praise for what in 1936?
   a. Civic humility.
   b. Fire prevention.
   c. Literate citizens.
   d. Sewage treatment.

**1930**

help: Search by phrase *national praise*

*Interior of Pasadena Civic Auditorium.*
*The Pasadena Civic Auditorium was built in 1932 in the Italian Renaissance style. The architects were Bergstrom, Bennett and Haskell. The chairs seen here are currently (2012) the chairs in the lecture room at the Pasadena Public Library Central Branch.*
*1932?*

*ppl_112*

133. In 1905, what did the Pasadena Humane Society find in the milk coming from Medici de Giron's cows?
   a. Arsenic.
   b. Bacteria.
   c. Formaldehyde.
   d. Old lace.

**1900**

help: *de Giron*


134. Rising prices of what raised the price of milk from to one to two cents in 1924?
   a. Buckets.
   b. Gasoline.
   c. Hay.
   d. Wages.

**1920**

help: Limit by date to 1924, then *milk*


135. A *Pasadena Weekly* article dated 06/09/2011 said that Caltech had produced ____ Nobel Prize winners since 1923?
   a. 15.
   b. 21.
   c. 31.
   d. 45.

help: Limit by date to 06/09/2011; limit by publication to *Pasadena Weekly* then *Nobel*


136. Mary Dell Baker died in 1931 when
   a. Her dress caught fire.
   b. Her car went over a cliff.
   c. Her gun went off.
   d. Her house blew up.

**1930**

help: *baker, Mary dell*

137. In March 1938, while Mrs. Myrle A. Dill was in jail as a suspect in an arson investigation
    a. Mr. Dill slept better.
    b. Mrs. Dill demanded her matches back.
    c. There was an outbreak of fires in the women's section of the jail.
    d. There were two new mystery fires outside the jail.

**1930**

help: *dill, Myrle a.*


138. (Fill in the blank.) Benjamin Chambers Brown donated some of his paintings to give aid to the _____ in 1917.
    a. Belgians.
    b. Dutch.
    c. French.
    d. Russians.

**1910**

help: Limit by date to 1917, then *brown, ben*


139. Like many other artists whose paintings now sell for lots of money, when he was alive, Benjamin Chambers Brown depended on who for sales?
    a. Investors.
    b. People of good taste.
    c. Rich people.
    d. Tourists.

help: *brown, ben* then *sales*

140. What type of Pasadena sport facility was displaced by $75,000 worth of fire damage in 1941?
   a. Basketball.
   b. Bowling.
   c. Dancing.
   d. Hockey.

**1940**

help: *fires* then *75,000*


141. According to an article in the February 5, 1914 issue of the Pasadena Star, in January 1914
   a. The number of library cards issued to men and women was about the same.
   b. Twice as many men as women got library cards.
   c. Twice as many women as men got library cards.

**1910**

help: Limit by date set to 02/05/1914, then *women*


142. Alice Barker was arrested in 1923 for being an alleged
   a. Arsonist.
   b. Fortune teller.
   c. Pain in the neck.
   d. Poisoner.

**1920**

help: *barker, Alice*


143. What was one of the more notable events at the Valley Hunt Club in 1962?
   a. An avowed Socialist playing tennis at the Club courts.
   b. The Club building a bigger clubhouse after a fire.
   c. A club member founding the Pasadena Opera Guild.
   d. The police raiding the club and arresting 4 men and 1 girl on the charge of gambling for the men and vice control for the girl.

**1960**

help: Limit by date to 1962, then *Valley Hunt*

144. Seen in 2011 at the Pasadena Civic Auditorium, "Real Love" was a
   a. Cat show.
   b. Health expo.
   c. New musical.
   d. Adult industry convention.

**2010**

help: *real love*


145. Oscar winning composer Marvin Hamlisch served as the conductor of the
   a. California Philharmonic.
   b. Pasadena POPS Orchestra.
   c. Pasadena Symphony Orchestra.
   d. Tuesday Musicale.

help: *Hamlisch* then *conductor*


146. The circus came to town (via Colorado Boulevard) from what country in 1916?
   a. China.
   b. Mexico.
   c. Russia.
   d. United States.

**1910**

help: *circus* then *Colorado*


147. In 1895 who led a field trip from Pasadena High School to the San Gabriel Mountains?
   a. Gifford Pinchot.
   b. John Muir.
   c. Theodore Parker Lukens.
   d. Theodore Roosevelt.

**1890**

help: *Pasadena High School* then *Mountains*

148. In 1942, the city had to install what to protect soldiers in front of the Constance Hotel?
Answer: _____ (Two words.)

**1940**

help: *Constance hotel* then *soldiers*


149. After William J. French, who had served as a lieutenant in the U.S. Army in World War One, was found dead in an auto wreck in 1932, it was reported that he might really have been:
   a. An enlisted man.
   b. A navy officer.
   c. A race car driver.
   d. An African-American man.

**1930**

help: *French, william J.*


150. When was the first Pasadena casualty (measured as an obituary) from the Vietnamese war reported in the *Pasadena Star-News*?
   a. 1964.
   b. 1965.
   c. 1966.
   d. 1967.

**1960**

help: Limit by article type to obituary, then *Vietnamese conflict* then scroll down to bottom of list.


151. Five planes were hired by the Forest Service to aid firefighters in the San Gabriel Mountains in what year?
   a. 1939.
   b. 1949.
   c. 1959.
   d. 1969.

help: Search by phrase *five planes*

152. A score (20) of firemen nearly died trying to save what in 1941?
   a. A bowling alley.
   b. A church.
   b. A kitten.
   c. An orphanage.

**1940**

help: Search by phrase *score of firemen*


153. Madeline Hitchcock was killed by cigarettes in 1941. She died from
   a. A car accident.
   b. A fire.
   c. Cancer.
   d. Nagging.

**1940**

help: *Hitchcock, M*


154. Lloyd's of London refused to sell insurance to the Tournament of Roses Association to protect them against bad what in 1918?
   a. Grandstand construction.
   b. Injuries.
   c. Parking.
   d. Weather.

**1910**

help: *Of roses, 1918* then *Lloyd*


155. What was seen as a notable feature to the 1918 Rose Bowl Game?
   a. Everyone but the special choir was to sing the National Anthem.
   b. Everyone was to know the words to the National Anthem.
   c. Everyone was to sing the National Anthem at the end of the game.
   d. Everyone was to sing the National Anthem at the start of the game.

**1910**

help: *1918 - Football game* then *national anthem*

156. Fill in the blank from this November 11, 1941, *Pasadena Star-News* headline, "Fire, poison, _____ on police list."
   a. Cars.
   b. Knives.
   c. Pistols.
   d. Radium.

help: Search by phrase *fire, poison*


157. Ruth Miller won a Silver Medal in the 1932 Olympics. She
   a. Won a medal for her painting of wrestling.
   b. Won a medal in wrestling.
   c. Won a medal in wrestling and had a painting made of it.

help: *Miller, Ruth* then *wrestling*


158. About how long did it take for the professional Los Angeles Dons (Football team) to get permission from the city to play in the Rose Bowl in the 1940's?
   a. Two hours.
   b. Two days.
   c. Two months.
   d. Two years.

help: *Los Angeles Dons (Football team)* then *application* (Make note of date) then *debut*


159. What kind of racing happened in the Arroyo Seco in 1928?
   a. Automobile.
   b. Dog.
   c. Duck.
   d. Motorcycle.

**1920**

help: *arroyo Seco* then *racing*

160. What kind of toy raced in the Arroyo Seco in 2011?
    a. Airplane.
    b. Car.
    c. Duck.
    d. Godzilla.

**2010**

help: *Arroyo Seco* then *toy*


161. (Fill in the blanks.) During World War Two, Elizabeth MacLean, Pasadena nurse, went to _____ where she served the _____ .
    a. Alaska/Eskimos.
    b. England/British.
    c. Japan/Japanese.
    d. Philippines/Filipinos.

**1940**

help: *maclean, El*


162. (Complete this sentence.) In October 1932, the Emergency Hospital saw someone who had been injured by the claws of a _____
    a. Cat.
    b. Duck.
    c. Monkey.
    d. Raccoon.

**1930**

help: *emergency hospital* then *claws*


163. E. Morley Brownscombe was saved by his what from a house fire in 1925?
    a. Cat.
    b. Dog.
    c. Horse.
    d. Monkey.

**1920**

help: *Brownscombe, E.*

164. A test revealed in 1939 that what aided fighting fires in the Angeles National Forest?
   a. Better parachutes.
   b. Bigger shovels.
   c. More water.
   d. Taller watch towers.

**1930**

help: Limit by date to 1939, then *Angeles National* then *test*


165. Erwin Smith died in 1942 at the Annandale Golf Club. He died from
   a. Burns caused by exploding gasoline.
   b. Drowning in a pond under mysterious circumstances.
   c. Heart attack making his first (and only) hole-in-one.
   d. Stroke brought on by his wife's play of bridge.

**1940**

help: *Smith, Erwin*


166. Which avowed Pasadena Socialist has been photographed at the Valley Hunt Club?
   a. Don Wheldon.
   b. Eugene Debs.
   c. J. J. Hicks.
   d. Upton Sinclair.

help: *valley hunt club* then *socialist*


167. Who defended Charles W. Paddock against "whispered charges" against his eligibility to participate in the 1928 Olympics?
   a. Albert Einstein.
   b. Douglas MacArthur.
   c. Errol Flynn.
   d. Franklin Roosevelt.

**1920**

help: *Paddock, Charles w.* then *whispered charges*

168. G. S. Parks said the City Council was "Unamerican" in 1928 because, in his view, it discriminated against
   a. African-Americans.
   b. Dogs.
   c. Veterans.
   d. Women.

**1920**

help: *Parks, g. S.*


169. When William Edward Hibbard, a prominent local physician who died in 1911 accidentally, his last thoughts were most likely, "Gee, I wish I had
   a. Gone nude to the bathroom."
   b. Learned how to dive, and more specifically corner, downhill."
   c. Walked a little further behind that horse on the Fourth of July."
   d. Worn smaller shoes while walking along that railroad track."

**1910**

help: *Hibbard, will*


170. After she won the high jump in the 1956 Olympics, Mildred Singleton was a
   a. Consultant for Avon Products.
   b. Manager for Orndoff Construction Company.
   c. Newspaper columnist for the *Pasadena Star-News*.
   d. Teacher at Charles W. Eliot Middle School.

**1950**

help: *singleton, mildred* then *won high jump*

*Pasadena City Hall Baseball Team - 1910*
*ppl_6232*

171. On Admission Day in 1890, the second library building at Walnut and Raymond was opened, and seven companies of the National Guard
    a. Annoyed patrons trying to read in quiet at the new public library.
    b. Tracked down for overdue books that had not been returned to the old public library
    c. Paraded to celebrate the opening of the new public library.
    d. Quelled the excessively rowdy patrons at the new public library.

**1890**

help: Limit by date to 1890, then *Admission Day*


172. At first they were disappointed I wasn't a fella,
    But after 300 floats and awards I can tell ya
    You stick flowers in water,
    And they last so much longer,
    And my first name is just Isabella.
    What is my last name?
Answer: _____

help: *floats* then *Isabella*


173. What is <u>not</u> true about the 1910 Pasadena Silk Stockings (Baseball baseball team). They
    a. Functioned as a farm team for the Vernon Tigers of the Pacific Coast League.
    b. Had a very cool name appropriate for Pasadena.
    c. Played at Brookside Park.
    d. Were a member of the Trolly Car League.

**1910**

help: *Pasadena silk Stockings*

174. In 1963, the 225 horses that were in the Rose Parade were valued at
   a. $35,000 ($262,000 in 2013 dollars or $1,164 a horse).
   b. $350,000 ($2,620,000 in 2013 dollars or $11,644 a horse).
   c. $3.5 million ($26,200,000 in 2013 dollars or $116,444 a horse).
   d. $35 million (260,000,000 in 2013 dollars or $1,164,444 a horse.)

**1960**

help: *of roses, 1963* then *horses*


175. Jackie Robinson was the batboy for which team?
   a. Pasadena Buicks.
   b. Pasadena Eagles.
   c. Pasadena Merchants.
   d. Pasadena Millionaires.

help: *Robinson, Jackie* then *batboy*


176. If you were reading a newspaper in 1907, you would be likely to know that a "gutta percha" was a
   a. Basketball hoop.
   b. Bird cage.
   c. Golf ball.
   d. Hitching post.

**1900**

help: Search by phrase *gutta percha*


177. Matthew Slavin thought that a union wage of _____ a day for a carpenter was too high in 1908.
   a. $1.75.
   b. $3.50.
   c. $4.25.
   d. $5.00.

**1900**

help: *Slavin* then *carpenter*

178. Rain forced what activity indoors to the lobby of the Huntington Hotel in 1920?
   a. Badminton.
   b. Golf.
   c. Horseshoes.
   d. Tennis.

help: *Huntington Hotel* then *lobby*


179. Phlunte Riddle was an African American trailblazer in which city department?
   a. City Attorney.
   b. Fire.
   c. Library.
   d. Police.

help: *Riddle, Ph* then *trailblazer*


180. In 2011, the California Philharmonic had a program Beethoven & _____
   a. Bossa Nova.
   b. Brahms.
   c. The Bangles.
   d. The Beatles.

help: Search by phrase *Beethoven &*


181. Evelyn Lindy Dewitt has been described as a "Mother." What has she been a mother to?
   a. Many, many athletes.
   b. Many, many cats.
   c. Many, many causes.
   d. Many, many girls.

help: *Dewitt, Evely*n then *mother*

182. In 2011 the musical group Freshlyground played at Memorial Park. They were from
   a. Brazil.
   b. Costa Rica.
   c. South Africa.
   d. Vietnam.

**2010**

help: *Freshlyground*


183. How many times has Michelle Obama visited Pasadena as of 2013?
   a. 0.
   b. 1.
   c. 2.
   d. 3.

help: *Obama, Michelle* then *visitors*


184. Charles Frederick Holder was there when what permanent organization was effected in 1897?
   a. Pasadena Academy of Sciences.
   b. Pasadena Art Association.
   c. Pasadena Medical Association.
   d. Pasadena Oratorio Society.

**1890**

help: *Holder, Charles Fred* then *effected*


185. David Paul Zimmerman, who was killed in Vietnam in 1968, was remembered as an
   a. Athlete.
   b. Comedian.
   c. Debater.
   d. Musician.

**1960**

help: *Zimmerman, david p*

186. (Fill in the blank.) At least from 1998-2012 in Pasadena we have a Christmas _____ Count
   a. Balloon.
   b. Bird.
   c. B-1 Bomber.
   d. RV.

help: *Christmas* then *count*


187. In 2012 scientists at Jet Propulsion Laboratory warned that something could paralyze our electrified world. Was it?
   a. Excessive texting.
   b. Global warming.
   c. Large earthquakes.
   d. Solar flares.

help: *Jet propulsion* then *electrified*


188. Courage, New Hampshire is produced in Pasadena. It is a
   a. Firearm.
   b. Graphic novel.
   c. Line of clothing.
   d. Television program.

help: *courage, new*


189. Alejandro Balazs at Caltech has been working on
   a. Gene splicing.
   b. Electric cars.
   c. HIV vaccines.
   d. Senior day pranks.

help: *Balazs,*

190. (Complete the phrase.) The television program Ben 10 Ultimate _____ is produced in Pasadena.
   a. Alien.
   b. Dog.
   c. Microbe.
   d. Zombie.

help: Search by phrase *Ben 10*


191. In 1962, George Herms put something so controversial in his art that was being exhibited by the Pasadena Museum of Art that someone felt like he had to break in and steal it, even though the Museum had already decided to withdraw it. The controversial thing was a
   a. Bible.
   b. Flag.
   c. Human body part.
   d. Representation of a human body part.

help: *herms, ge* then *withdraw*


192. In what year did students get an eight-foot zone of safety for getting in cars at Pasadena High School?
   a. 1916.
   b. 1946.
   c. 1976.
   d. 2006.

help: Search by phrase *eight-foot*

*Interior of 2nd Pasadena Public Library Central bldg, Reading room. 1900?*

*ppl_148*

193. $180 ($2,450 in 2013 dollars) a day would get you what in 1928?
   a. A very nice hotel room.
   b. Clean streets.
   c. Decent schools.
   d. Drinkable water.

**1920**

help: Search by phrase *180* then *day*


194. Preaching a sermon in 1906, Frank M. Dowling of the First Christian Church said that the "beginning" was how long ago?
   a. The blink of an eye.
   b. 1,800 years.
   c. 6,000 years.
   d. 50,000 years.

**1900**

help: *Dowling* then *beginning*


195. What was the climax to the Big Week at Pasadena High School in October, 1924? Did they
   a. Burn some garbage on Colorado Boulevard?
   b. Listen to a speech by Charles Paddock?
   c. Stack a bunch of cheerleaders in the gym?
   d. Overturn cars in the faculty parking lot?

**1920**

help: Search by phrase phrase *big week*


196. What was the most pressing need of the Pasadena Public Library in 1915?
   a. Books.
   b. Lighting.
   c. Parking.
   d. Space.

**1910**

help: *Pasadena public library* then *pressing*

197. (Fill in the blank.) When Herbert Hoover campaigned in Pasadena in 1928 to be president, he was allowed a full _____ to address the crowd.
    a. 5 minutes.
    b. 10 minutes.
    c. 2 hours.
    d. What seemed like eternity.

**1920**

help: *Hoover, herb* then *allowed full*


198. The headline that began "Women scantily clad" in 1912 referred to a
    a. Beach outing by girls without their parents.
    b. Fire at the La Pintoresca hotel.
    c. Rally for women's suffrage.
    d. Wild party in the Arroyo.

**1910**

help: Search by phrase *women scantily clad*


199. How many people died in 1896 when a Chinese wash house burned down?
a. 0.
b. 1.
c. 2.
d. 5.

**1890**

help: Search by phrase *Chinese wash house*


200. Before she ordered around clerks as a 2nd Lieutenant in the Army during World War Two, Florence Lormer ordered around
    a. Patients as a nurse at Huntington Hospital.
    b. Patrons as a librarian at Pasadena Public Library (nicely, of course).
    c. Pedestrians as a policewoman for the Pasadena Police Department.
    d. Pupils as a teacher at Henry Wadsworth Longfellow Elementary School.

**1940**

help: *Lormer*

201. On Opening Day of the Mount Lowe Railway, one of the guests was Jason Brown, who fought against slavery before the Civil War with his father John Brown, although he was not at Harper's Ferry. What was most notable about his appearance at the event?
    a. He gave a speech talking about the Civil War.
    b. He walked to the dedication site.
    c. He was bitten by a bear.
    d. He was honored by the African-American community.

help: *Mount Lowe Railway* then *Opening Day*


202. I won one for the Gipper,
    And two for the White House,
    And as a TV actor one year I checked out a float.
    What is my last name?
Answer: _____

help: *float* then *TV actor*


203. It was announced in 1924 that The Pasadena Grand Opera House on Raymond Avenue was going to be torn down to make room for what?
    a. Chaffee's Grand Central Market.
    b. The Raymond Theater.
    c. The Royal Laundry.
    d. The Theosophical Library Center.

**1920**

help: Limit by date to 1924 then *Pasadena grand opera house*

*Built in 1889 at a cost of $100,000, the Pasadena Grand Opera House had a seating capacity of 1500. The building was razed in 1923. This is a view of the front facade which faced Raymond Avenue and the side view from Bellview Drive. 1898?*

                          *ppl_105*

204. In 2005, The Royal Laundry Building, which had replaced the Pasadena Grand Opera House on South Raymond, had a new tenant. Was it
   a. Art Center College of Design.
   b. The Disney Store.
   c. The Pasadena Humane Society.
   d. The Postal Service.

**2000**

help: Limit by date to 2005, then *Royal Laundry building*


205. In July 1945, to support an anticipated need by returning veterans from World War Two, the City Council (then called the Board of Directors) decided to not tax
   a. Adaptive devices on automobiles.
   b. Hotel stays for visiting relatives.
   c. Guide dogs for the blind.
   d. Marriage licenses for war brides.

**1940**

help: Limit by date to July 1945, then *1939-1945* then *directors*


206. Pasadena City College teams are now known as the Lancers. Between 1931 and 1932, Pasadena Junior College teams, like track, were known as the
   a. Basset Hounds.
   b. Beagles.
   c. Boxers.
   d. St. Bernards.

**1930**

help: Limit by date from 1931 to 1932, then *Pasadena Junior College* then *track*

*1st Class. School of Theatre. Pasadena Community Playhouse Association.*
*Founder of the Playhouse, Gilmor Brown, seems to be the gentleman in the center of the photo.*
*1928?*

ppl_6512

207. Pasadena City College teams are now known as the Lancers. Between 1933 and 1935, Pasadena Junior College teams were known as the
   a. Malteses.
   b. Mastiffs.
   c. Mexican Hairlesses.
   d. Mongrels.

**1930**

help: Limit by date from 1933 to 1935, then *Pasadena Junior College* then *track*


208. In 1932, seven Pasadena Junior College students were jailed for throwing what at police?
   a. Snowballs.
   b. Spit-wads.
   c. Sticks.
   d. Stones.

**1930**

help: Limit by date to 1932, then *Pasadena Junior college* then *jailed*


209. How many brick buildings were there on Colorado Boulevard in 1883?
   a. 0.
   b. 1.
   c. 2.
   d. 5.

**1890**

help: *Colorado Bo* then *brick*


210. In 1938, the Pasadena Playhouse's production of what was approaching the thousand mark?
   a. Actors.
   b. Costumes.
   c. Plays.
   d. Sets.

**1930**

help: *Pasadena Playhouse* then *thousand mark*

211. Very briefly in 1944, Devil's Gate Dam was renamed to honor what engineer?
    a. George K. Hooper.
    b. Herbert Hoover.
    c. James W. Reagan.
    d. Samuel B. Morris.

**1940**

help: *Gate* then *dam name*


212. Linda Peterson was 3 years old when she died in 1958. Her death led to a crackdown on
a. Unlocked handguns.
b. Unsecured refrigerators.
c. Unleashed dogs.
d. Unvaccinated children.

**1950**

help: *Peterson, Linda* then *crackdown*


213. In 1915, which group asked that parts of the movie now called "Birth of a Nation" be eliminated before the film was shown in Pasadena?
    a. Ku Klux Klan.
    b. Negro Taxpayers' and Voters' Association of Pasadena.
    c. Orange Grove Meeting of the Religious Society of Friends.
    d. Shakespeare Club.

**1910**

help: *Birth of a Nation* then *eliminated*


214. In the 19th Century, one pricey piano was involved in what kind of "deal"?
a. Land.
b. Money-Back.
c. Technically legal but morally suspect.
d. Water.

help: search by phrase *one pricey piano*

215. (Fill in the blank from this 1999 *Pasadena Star-News* headline.) "Lake Avenue Church's music pastoral thrills _____ with orchestral arrangements of country's national anthem."
   a. Laotians.
   b. Lebanese.
   c. Liberians.
   d. Lithuanians.

**1990**

help: Search by phrase *music pastor thrills*


216. According to a 1988 editorial in the *Pasadena Star-News*, Joe Coulombe, founder of Trader Joe's, does marketing with a
   a. Sigh.
   b. Smile.
   c. Smirk.
   d. Sneer.

**1980**

help: *Coulombe* then *marketing*


217. According to an editorial in the *Pasadena Star-News*, in what year was it announced that "911 a number that could change your life"?
   a. 1964.
   b. 1974.
   c. 1984.
   d. 1994.

help: Search by phrase *911 a number*

*Pacific Telephone Building located on 17 East Colorado Blvd. View is of front of the building facing Arroyo Pkwy. Pacific Telephone logo on brick wall in front of building. It is currently (2013) known as the AT&T Building.*

*ppl_8385*

218. Between 2003 and 2006, Parsons Corporation received contracts to rebuild everything in Iraq except
    a. Airports.
    b. Colleges.
    c. Oil refineries.
    d. Police buildings.

help: Limit by date from 2003 to 2006 then *Parsons Corporation* then *Iraq*

219. What part of the African American Community was organized on South Raymond Avenue in 1918?
    a. An auxiliary of the American Red Cross.
    b. An auxiliary of the Pasadena Grand Opera.
    c. An auxiliary of the Pasadena Humane Society.
    d. An auxiliary of the Pasadena Lawn Bowling Club.

help: *african americans* then *Raymond avenue*

220. In 1918, how many members of the African American community were drafted in the Army and ordered to Camp Lewis?
    a. 0.
    b. 7.
    c. 14.
    d. 21.

help: Limit date to 1918, then *african Americans* then *camp Lewis*

221. In 1928 at the Raymond Hotel, the Americans defeated British in
    a. Chess.
    b. Croquet.
    c. Golf.
    d. Lawn bowling.

help: *Raymond Hotel* then *British*

*Colorado Street*
This photo shows a vibrant day on Colorado Boulevard some time between 1888 and 1893. Looking east from the intersection of Colorado Boulevard and Fair Oaks Avenue, a precise date cannot be found due to a lack of detailed records. The San Gabriel Valley Bank, the building to the far right, was organized in February 1886 and moved to this location in 1887. A gas street lamp is also prominently displayed in the center of the photo as it hangs over Colorado Boulevard.

*ppl_5027*

222. For Christmas in 1965, girls in Pasadena called GIs in
   a. Germany.
   b. Glendale.
   c. Korea.
   d. Vietnam.

**1960**

help: Limit by date to 1965, then search by phrase *girls*


223. On January 6, 1984, 911 service was introduced with the headline "Call 911…but only for emergency needs." When was the headline "Police report first abuse of 911 system" written?
   a. January 8, 1984.
   b. January 12, 1984.
   c. February 3, 1984.
   d. February 21, 1984.

**1980**

help: Search by phrase *911* then *first abuse*


224. On January 6, 1984, 911 service was introduced with the headline "Call 911…but only for emergency needs." When was the headline "Woman arrested for misuse of 911 system" written?
   a. January 12, 1984
   b. February 21, 1984.
   c. March 3, 1984.
   d. January 18, 1985.

**1980**

help:Search by phrase *911* then *woman arrested*

225. The "California Tech Yacht Club"
   a. Has committed several act of piracy against its arch-rival, the Massachusetts Tech Yacht Club.
   b. Is a distinctive T-shirt that can be purchased at the Caltech Bookstore.
   c. Periodically comes into existence during and after a heavy rainstorm along Wilson Avenue.
   d. Was the sponsoring organization for an Olympic yachter, Frank Jewett, in the 1936 Olympics.

help: Search by phrase *tech yacht club*


226. People Inside Electronics is a
   a. Co-ed technology education group.
   b. Hackers group.
   c. Musical group.
   d. Tron movie fan group.

help: *People inside electronics*


227. Hobbits had a convention at the Pasadena Center in what year?
   a. 1975.
   b. 1985.
   c. 1995.
   d. 2005.

help: Search by phrase *hobbits*


228. Larry Tatum taught kids to kick-start their self-esteem by teaching them to
   a. Climb things.
   b. Jump out of things.
   c. Kick things.
   d. Say nice things.

help: *Tatum, larry* then *kick-start*

229. In 2010, Ruben Hernandez used voodoo to
   a. Ensure that USC would beat UCLA in football.
   b. Find a wife who would love him for the "Inner Ruben."
   c. Punish police who had arrested him for fraud.
   d. Silence a neighbor's dog that was keeping him up at night.

**2010**

help: *Hernandez,* then *voodoo*


230. In 1927, C.V. Cowan, city reviewer, claimed to have viewed eighteen million feet of film to protect Pasadena from things that should't be seen. If 16 frames are in a foot of film, and film projects at 24 frames a second, and a work day consists of 8 hours, what can we assume about Mr. Cowan?
   a. He put in a lot of overtime.
   b. He really liked his job.
   c. He wasn't known for his tan or manly physique.
   d. His boss probably should have paid more attention.
   e. All of the above.

**1920**

help: I used a calculator


231. The 1929 motion picture "Godless Girl" had 70 feet cut from it because it showed too much what for Pasadenans?
   a. Drinking.
   b. Indecency.
   c. Smoking.
   d. Swearing.

**1920**

help: Search by phrase *Godless Girl*

232. I thought that only 6000 would see me, but 7400 showed up,
   I brought back a temple bell from Japan after the war,
   The City Manager spoke when I was born.
   What am I?
Answer: _____

**1940**

help: Search by phrase *7400*


233. Fill in the blank from this front page headline from the April 12, 1902 *Pasadena Daily News* about Mollie Forrest: "Mock _____, Blighted Love, Heart Broken: Young woman tells story of suffering."
   a. Courage.
   b. Marriage.
   c. Orange.
   d. Words.

**1900**

help: Search by phrase *blighted love*


234. (Fill in the blank.) In 1928, Norman Kling, Chicago Baritone, sang at the _____ Tabernacle in Pasadena
   a. Hawaiian.
   b. Lithuanian.
   c. Mormon.
   d. Swedish.

**1920**

help: *Kling, no*

235. In 1928, the motion picture "Olympic Hero" had some scenes with Olympic star Charles W. Paddock. The movie
   a. Co-starred fellow Pasadena Olympian Lillian Copeland.
   b. Had several scenes of him running on the beach, in slow motion.
   c. Nearly cost Charles W. Paddock his amateur status in the 1928 Olympic games.
   d. Was produced to promote Charles W. Paddock as the next Tarzan.

**1920**

help: *Olympic hero (motion picture)*


236. Complete this headline from the January 26, 1912 *Pasadena Daily News*: "Bad luck clings: J. Jacobson, victim of recent fire, loses another _____"
   a. Barn.
   b. Car.
   c. Horse.
   d. Wife.

**1910**

help: *Jacobson, J.*


237. Because the elections would be "too costly," in 1948, the City Council denied the request by the Native Sons and Daughters of the Golden West to have an election on the City's proposal to do what?
   a. Force citizens to sing hymns at the altar the Great God Meter.
   b. Have certain zones be mandatory paid parking 24/7.
   c. Put in parking meters.
   d. Require coins used to feed parking meters be clean.

**1940**

help: *of the golden west* then *too costly*

238. In 1910, to play in a grammar school baseball league, players had to promise not to
   a. Cheat.
   b. Drink alcohol.
   c. Swear.
   d. Use tobacco.

**1910**

help: Search by phrase *grammar school baseball*


239. Lake Avenue Congregational Church was 100 years old in
   a. 1993.
   b. 1996.
   c. 2003.
   d. 2006.

help: *Lake Avenue Cong* then *100 years*


240. Montague Glass was a famous Pasadena author and playwright. In 1926 he was arrested for
   a. Jaywalking.
   b. Loitering.
   c. Littering.
   d. Parking illegally, a lot.

**1920**

help: *Glass, Mont*


241. The Arroyo Anachrist was
   a. A caped crusader for Communism.
   b. A dog that won best of breed at the Westminster Dog show.
   c. A performance artist who performed in the flood control channel.
   d. Fomer Pasadena Mayor Rick Cole.

help: *Arroyo Anarchist*

242. In order to save the city money in 1912, C. Wellington Koiner, manager of the Municipal Light Plant, had an idea for an alternate fuel for autos. Was it
   a. Electricity.
   b. Coal.
   c. Natural gas.
   d. Wood.

**1910**

help: Limit by date to 1912, then *Koiner, C.*


243. The prospect of doing "road work" in the Arroyo Seco drew what boxing great to stay in Pasadena in 1939?
   a. Joe Louis.
   b. Max Baer.
   c. Max Schmeling.
   d. Tony Canzoneri.

**1930**

help: *boxing* then *road work*


244. When Olympic spirnter Charles W. Paddock lost "Rusty" in 1928, he offered a reward. Rusty was his
   a. Car.
   b. Dog.
   c. Rabbit's foot.
   d. Watch.

**1920**

help: *paddock* then *Rusty*

*Unidentified man with dogs.*
*ppl_8771*

245. In 1904, Mr. William Cairns, Jr., abandoned his wife Mrs. William Cairns, Jr., "without a word and without a cent." Mrs. Cairns blamed
   a. Mr. Cairns.
   b. Mr. Cairns' mother.
   c. Mr. Cairns' shameless hussy of a secretary.
   d. Mrs. Cairns' mother.

**1900**

help: *Cairns* then *without a cent*


246. In March 1902, members of what ethnic group were arrested for not having their "papers" in Pasadena?
   a. Chinese.
   b. Japanese.
   c. Mexican.
   d. Filipino.

**1900**

help: limit by date to March 1902 then search by phrase *papers*


247. At one point in the 1920's, the Boy Scouts had a camp on what island?
   a. Anacapa.
   b. Catalina.
   c. Gilligan's.
   d. Hawaii.

**1920**

help: *Boy Scouts* then *island*


248. Students from Mayfield Junior School got to ride in a helicopter in 2000 because they
   a. Assisted the Police Department in Operation Santa.
   b. Got lost in the mountains.
   c. Trounced Poly in volleyball.
   d. Won the lottery.

**2000**

help: *Mayfield Junior* then *hel*

249. By lecturing to Boy Scouts about birds in 1919, the Audubon Society sought to counteract the effects of
   a. Hunting.
   b. Modern life.
   c. Racism.
   d. War.

**1910**

help: *boy scouts* then *Audubon*


250. William Lewis Halbe was shot and killed during a raid on a poker game in 1924. The police chief demanded an investigation by a grand jury because he was shot by
   a. An African-American.
   b. A fireman.
   c. A sheriff's deputy.
   d. A woman.

**1920**

help: *Halbe* then *jury holds*


251. What was told to be silent by the City Council in 1931 on Colorado Boulevard?
   a. Car horns.
   b. Horses.
   c. Street vendors.
   d. Traffic signals.

**1930**

help: *Colorado Boul* then *silent*

252. In 1953, angry citizens complained about City Manager Don C. McMillan's golf game. They thought he played too
   a. Little.
   b. Much.
   c. Poorly.
   d. Well.

**1950**

help: *city manager* then *golf*


253. John M. McCarthy was put in charge of Saint Andrew's Church in 1918 after twenty years in
   a. Fresno.
   b. New York.
   c. Columbus.
   d. San Francisco.

**1910**

help: *McCarthy, john M.* then *twenty years*


254. TNT was the nickname for
   a. Canuto Robledo (boxer).
   b. L. A. Dacey (contractor).
   c. Robert Wiseman (bookie).
   d. William Cottrell (arsonist).

help: Search by phrase *TNT*


255. According to a 1923 *Pasadena Star-News* article, Chihuahita, a Mexican colony in Pasadena, was established by
   a. Abbott Kinney.
   b. Henry Huntington.
   c. Lucky Baldwin.
   d. Matthew Slavin.

**1920**

help: *Chihua* then *was estab*

256. (Fill in the blank from this 2010 Pasadena Weekly headline.) Dengue Fever blends _____ and American rock at the Levitt (in Memorial Park).
   a. Australian.
   b. Cambodian.
   c. Nigerian.
   d. Panamanian.

**2010**

help: *Dengue Fever* then *blends*


257. When Hillary Rodham Clinton visited Pasadena for a low-key fundraiser for the election in 2008, where did it take place?
   a. La Casita del Arroyo.
   b. The home of Maurice Thomas Morse.
   c. The Hotel Green.
   d. Twin Palms Restaurant.

**2000**

help: *Clinton, Hillary* then *low-key*


258. I taught art at Pasadena Poly High School
   I served in the military in the Second World War
   My first name was Milford
   What is my last name?
   Answer: _____

**1940**

help: *Pasadena poly high* then *milford*

*Drawing Room. East Hall Throop Polytechnic Institute, Pasadena, California.
Caltech was founded in 1891 under the name of Throop University. In 1892 the school was renamed Throop Polytechnic Institute, and in 1913 Throop Institute of Technology. In 1920 the current name of California Institute of Technology was applied to the school.*

*ppl_3866*

259. Ko Yomagashi was the second what in January 1945?
   a. Second Japanese American to be enrolled in a Pasadena school after evacuation.
   b. Second Japanese American to be hired by the city after evacuation.
   c. Second Japanese American to reopen his business in Pasadena after evacuation.
   d. Second Japanese American to return to Pasadena after evacuation.

**1940**

help: *evacuation* then *Yoma*


260. All of this is true about Thomas Kral EXCEPT
   a. He was an actor who became a writer/director.
   b. Later in his career he became a producer.
   c. His work was seen at the Pasadena Playhouse.
   d. He wrote an all-GI musical comedy at the end of World War Two.

**1940**

help: *Kral, Thomas*


261. In the 1940's, the Pasadena Panthers who played teams like the Hollywood Wolves were a
   a. Bowling team.
   b. Football team.
   c. Hockey team.
   d. Softball team.

**1940**

help: *Pasadena panthers* then *hollywood wolves*

262. In 2011, a local post office on Colorado Boulevard was named after Oliver Goodall, an African American. Mr. Goodall was a
   a. Bay City Roller.
   b. Four Top.
   c. Kansas City Monarch.
   d. Tuskegee Airman.

**2010**

help: *Goodall, Oliver* then *postal service*


263. What type of books were in great demand at the Pasadena Public Library in 1914?
   a. Classic.
   b. Comic.
   c. Modern.
   d. Naughty.

**1910**

help: *Pasadena Public Library* then *great demand*


264. Barbara Bennett's girlish dreams came true when she was rescued by 1920's heartthrob
   a. Babe Ruth.
   b. Charles Lindbergh.
   c. F. Scott Fitzgerald.
   d. Rudolph Valentino.

**1920**

help: *Bennett, Barbara*


265. People living at 3600 Rams Top Road found what in their swimming pool in 2009?
   a. A bear.
   b. A mountain lion.
   c. A person trying to get to the Rose Bowl.
   d. An excessive amount of soot.

**2000**

help: *Rams Top Road*

266. The Library Board in Pasadena has been discussing the "wheel-chair problem" since
   a. 1900.
   b. 1920.
   c. 1950.
   d. 1990.

help: Search by phrase *wheel-chair problem*


267. Betty Scott, a student from Pasadena Junior College, died in 1944 in the Army as a WASP. WASP stands for
   a. Women Auxiliary Support Physicians.
   b. Women Amphibious Status Plotters.
   c. Women Airforce Service Pilots.
   d. Women Army Supply Personnel.

help: *Scott, Betty* then *WASP*


268. Engineers from Caltech in May 1924 did what to the Linda Vista Bridge?
   a. Blew it up.
   b. Built it.
   c. Designed it.
   d. Pranked it.

help: *California Ins* then *Linda Vista bridge*


269. Alumni of which Pasadena high school were on the USS Pueblo in 1966?
   a. Blair.
   b. John Marshall.
   c. John Muir.
   d. Pasadena.

help: *pueblo* then *high school*

270. Lillie A. Colby was a former actress who owned a camp in the San Gabriel Mountains. She died there in 1927 because she got close to
    a. Cold.
    b. Flames.
    c. Rocks.
    d. Water.

**1920**

help: Limit by article type to obituary, then *Colby, Lillie*


271. (Fill in the blank.) Appointed in 2010, Philip L. Sanchez was Pasadena's _____ Latino Chief of Police.
a. First.
b. Second.
c. Third.
d. Fourth.

help: *Sanchez, Phil* then *latino*


272. When actor Gary Coleman died in 2010, he willed his _____ collection to a Pasadena store
    a. Coin.
    b. Costume.
    b. Gun.
    d. Toy train.

help: *Coleman, Gary*


273. Canuto Robledo was a boxing trainer who was disabled in what way?
    a. Blindness.
    b. Deafness.
    c. Mute.
    d. Missing a limb.

help: *Robledo* then *disabled*

274. Rose Gudiel was upset to the point of inciting demonstrations from 2011-2012 because she thought
    a. Her bank had mishandled her loan.
    b. Her neighbors had too many animals.
    c. Her son was still living at home.
    d. Her sidewalk was too bumpy.

**2010**

help: *Gudiel, Rose*


275. A game other than football was called,
So they found one with a ball six feet tall.
And so in 1909,
The tournament thought it was just fine,
In a New Year's game of push _____
Answer: _____

**1900**

help: *1909* then *push*


276. Why was the city "practically deserted" in 1908?
    a. The flood waters were too high.
    b. The germs were too virulent.
    c. The Navy was in port.
    d. The weather was too hot.

**1900**

help: Search by phrase *practically deserted*

*Service revolver practice at Pasadena Police Department's Eaton Canyon shooting range.*
*ppl_13157*

277. In 1931 diligent police work by Cecil H. Burlingame and Harry B. Cheek determined that the supposed burglar who entered through the broken window was in fact a
   a. Cat.
   b. Dog.
   c. Monkey.
   d. Quail.

**1930**

help: *Burlingame, Cecil* then *cheek, Harry*


278. What organization, which opposed Al Smith for President because he favored the repeal of Prohibition, was said to be reorganizing in Pasadena in 1928?
   a. Ku Klux Klan.
   b. United Church Brotherhood.
   c. New Century Club.
   d. Women's Christian Temperance Union.

**1920**

help: *Elections, 1928* then *Smith*


279. In 1928, the Pasadena Police Department came in second in a national competition involving
   a. Driving.
   b. Eating.
   c. Running.
   d. Shooting.

**1920**

help: Limit date to 1928, then *police department* then *second*

280. If you had been going north on Arroyo Parkway, then called Broadway, on a Friday in August 1928, what have likely have delayed your trip?
   a. People escorting circus animals across the street.
   b. People gawking at the building built along the street.
   c. People listening to a campaign rally in the street.
   d. People trying to figure out the new parking system on the street.

**1920**

help: Limit by date to August 1928 then *Arroyo Parkway*


281. To raise money to help fight World War One, boys in Boy Scout Troop 8 in October 1918 raised how much in one week in 2013 dollars?
   a. $240.
   b. $2,400.
   c. $3,710.
   d. $37,100.

**1910**

help: Limit by date to October 1918, then *Boy Scouts* then Google *current value of a dollar* and convert at website like http://www.measuringworth.com/uscompare/


282. In 2003, how many members of Troop 35 at Mayfield Junior School made Eagle Scout?
   a. 5.
   b. 8.
   c. 11.
   d. 14.

**2000**

help: Search by phrase *troop 35*

283. In 1938 an Indian burial ground was discovered near Sheldon Reservoir. Richard Curtis, age 11, helped at the site and uncovered one of the skeletons. He got to name it and he called it
   a. Logi.
   b. Mogi.
   c. Bones.
   d. Yogi.

**1930**

help: *Curtis, Richard*


284. In 1945, women bankers were shown how to do what at Pasadena Junior College?
   a. Change a tire.
   b. Put on makeup.
   c. Speak Spanish.
   d. Transition out of the workforce.

**1940**

help: Search by phrase *women bankers*


285. In 1948, at age 80, Bessie Lee Cowie, an abolitionist, wanted to become a
   a. City Council Member.
   b. Judge.
   c. Librarian.
   d. Policewoman.

**1940**

help: Limit by date to 1948, then *Cowie,*


286. In 1918, during World War One, women from Pasadena went to Hemet to
   a. Care for orphans.
   b. Entertain troops.
   c. Pick fruit.
   d. Wrap bandages.

**1910**

help: *women* then *Hemet*

287. Which television program, set in New York, has used Pasadena as a film location?
   a. Dick Van Dyke Show.
   b. I Love Lucy.
   c. Mad Men.
   d. Ugly Betty.

help: *location* then *New York*


288. Fireman Wendell Eaton got to participate in which reality TV program when it filmed at a Pasadena location in 2013?
   a. America's Got Talent.
   b. Dirty Jobs.
   c. Fear Factor.
   d. MasterChef.

**2010**

help: *Eaton, We*


289. Although it usually banned such films, in 1933 the City Board of Review received a plea to run the motion picture "Elysia" because of its pro-what viewpoint?
   a. Communist.
   b. Nihilist.
   c. Nudist.
   d. Veganist.

**1930**

help: *elysia*

290. In 1967, Laurel L. Buckle sought to support the troops in Vietnam in their battle against
   a. Boredom.
   b. Disease.
   c. Fear.
   d. Poor food.

**1960**

help: *Buckle, L*


291. Harold E. Morris died in the Battle of Bougainville (1943-1945). His father, Clarence H. Morris, later became
   a. Fire chief.
   b. Mayor.
   c. Police chief.
   d. Superior court judge.

**1940**

help: *Morris, Clarence*


292. For the 1976 Rose Parade, the Rose Court did what by the numbers?
   a. Dance.
   b. Dress.
   c. Smile.
   d. Wave.

**1970**

help: *1976 - Queen and* then *numbers*


293. The first Major League baseball team to be mentioned in the newspapers as being interested in Pasadena as a site for spring training (1910) was
   a. The Boston Americans.
   b. The Chicago Cubs.
   c. The Chicago White Sox.
   d. The Pittsburgh Pirates.

**1910**

help: *baseball team* then *spring training* then scroll down to *1910*

294. In 1910, the first Major League baseball team to break the hearts of people in Pasadena by not showing up to play their scheduled game at Tournament Park was
    a. The Boston Americans.
    b. The Chicago Cubs.
    c. The Chicago White Sox.
    d. The Pittsburgh Pirates.

**1910**

help: Limit by date to 1910, then *baseball team* then *tournament park*


295. The first Major league baseball team to actually have a "winter quarters" (spring training) in Pasadena (1917) was
    a. The Boston Americans.
    b. The Chicago Cubs.
    c. The Chicago White Sox.
    d. The Pittsburgh Pirates.

**1910**

help: Limit by date to 1917, then *baseball team* then *quarters*


296. Angered that something of his had been stolen in 1926, police officer Marion Weimer Pursell called out the entire police force to hunt for it. The stolen item was his
    a. Automobile.
    b. Son's bicycle.
    c. Wife' engagement ring.
    d. Watermelon.

**1920**

help: *Pursell, Mar*

*Chicago White Sox Spring Training at Brookside Park in 1938 A series of photos probably taken on Wednesday March 9, 1938, when 'a field day for cameramen' was held.*

                *ppl_5301*

297. In 1984, the City Council decided that Michael Jackson was loud rock and roll, and therefore not appropriate for the Rose Bowl. Where did Michael Jackson play in the LA area that year?
   a. Dodger Stadium.
   b. The Big A.
   c. The Coliseum.
   d. The Fabulous Forum.

**1980**

help: Limit by date to 1984, then *Jackson, Michael* then *city council*


298. Did Michael Jackson ever perform in Pasadena?
   a. No.
   b. Yes.

help: *Jackson, Michael* then *visitors*


299. Pastor Lucious W. Smith spoke at Michael Jackson's memorial service and became a "star". He was a pastor at which Pasadena church in 2009?
   a. First African Methodist Episcopal Church.
   b. Friendship Baptist Church.
   c. Morning Star Baptist Church.
   d. Victory Bible Full Gospel Baptist Church.

**2000**

help: *Smith, Lu* then *Jackson*


300. Mike Fanous, a security guard at the Pasadena Public Library, and his son Jessi like to work together with
   a. Gears and oil.
   b. Spokes and wheels.
   c. Sticks and balls.
   d. Wood and boards.

help: *Fanous, Mike*

301. I made a Central Library frieze
of a boy who does what he please
My first name is Maude
My sculptures were quite Mod
and my middle initial is the letter _____
Answer: _____

help: *maude* then *frieze*


302. What did Girl Scout Katie Caswell use in the Huntington Hospital in 2004?
   a. A book cart.
   b. A dog leash.
   c. A paintbrush.
   d. A serving tray.

help: *Caswell, K*


303. According to the Pasadena Evening Star, Frank T. Kuranaga lost "A Big Fortune" in the San Francisco Earthquake of 1906. Again, according to the Pasadena Evening Star, about how much did Mr. Kuranaga lose (in 2013 dollars)?
   a. $1,000,000.
   b. $4,000,000.
   c. $8,000,000
   d. $12,000,000.

**1900**

help: *Kuranaga* then *big fortune* then Google current value of a dollar, then convert at a web site like measuringworth.com/uscompare

304. According to the Pasadena Star in 1914, Mrs. Leaonna Kuranaga wanted a divorce from Mr. Frank Kuranaga because he
   a. Already had a mother; she was not another.
   b. Had become poor; she preferred not to be.
   c. Had one way to educate their daughter; she had another.
   d. Was Japanese; she was not.

**1910**

help: *Kuranaga* then *divorce*


305. Which famous comedian died in Pasadena at Las Encinas Hospital in 1946?
   a. Buster Keaton.
   b. Groucho Marx.
   c. Richard Jeni.
   d. W. C. Fields.

**1940**

help: Limit by article type to obituaries; date to 1946, then *Las Encinas*


306. In 2002, Daisies from Mayfield Junior School
   a. Painted daisies.
   b. Planted daisies.
   c. Played daisies.
   d. Propelled daisies.

**2000**

help: *Mayfield J* then *daisies*


307. In 1928, some parents at Grover Cleveland Elementary School requested segregation from which group of children
   a. African American.
   b. Japanese American.
   c. Jewish.
   d. Mexican American.

**1920**

help: *Grover Cleveland* then *segregation*

308. Neil Clisby was an African American who got his picture in the newspaper in 1928 because
   a. He knew how to throw a good punch.
   b. He looked good in a military uniform.
   c. His academic record was very, very good.
   d. His voice sounded good over the radio.

**1920**

help: *Clisby, N*


309. (Fill in the blank.) In 1946 a patient at McCornack General Hospital (formerly the Vista Del Arroyo Hotel and now the home on the 9th Circuit Court of Appeals) was both a veteran of World War Two and a royal _____ Prince.
   a. Dutch.
   b. Japanese.
   c. Polish.
   d. Thai.

**1940**

help: *McCornack* then *Royal*


310. (Fill in the blank.) In 2007, the Girl Scouts celebrated their _____ anniversary in Pasadena.
   a. 55th.
   b. 75th.
   c. 95th.
   d. 115th.

**2000**

help: Limit by date to 2007, then *Girl Scouts* then *anniversary*

311. When were the first trees taken down because they got in the way on Colorado Boulevard?
   a. 1915.
   b. 1922.
   c. 1926.
   d. 1935.

help: *Colorado Boul* then *trees* then scroll down to the bottom of the list.

312. When was the first editorial suggesting that trees on Colorado were a commendable (good) idea
   a. 1915.
   b. 1922.
   c. 1926.
   d. 1935.

help: Limit by article type to editorial, then *Colorado Boul* then *trees*

313. Patti Patton-Badder, America's favorite mom, and her organization have sent care packages to troops in Iraq starting in 2004. Her organization is called Soldiers' _____ ?
   a. Angels.
   b. Delivery.
   c. Hearts.
   d. Mission.

**2000**

help: *der, patti* then *sold*

The Maryland Hotel on Colorado between Euclid and Los Robles 1915?

*ppl_4096*

314. Governor Schwarzenegger lauded a Pasadena Marine for his service in Iraq after his death in 2007. The marine, Rogelio Ramirez, attended which high school in Pasadena?
   a. Blair.
   b. John Marshall.
   c. John Muir.
   d. Pasadena.

2000

help: *Ramirez, Rogelio* then *high school*


315. Before the invasion of Iraq in 2003, the Pasadena City Council
   a. Did not pass an anti-war resolution.
   b. Did not pass a pro-war resolution.
   c. Passed an anti-war resolution.
   d. Passed a pro-war resolution.

2000

help: Limit date to 2003, then *Iraq* then *resolution*


316. Patrick Briggs and Mary Gavel-Briggs were sued by the city for having something that the city thought was the wrong size on their property in 2005. The offending item was a _____.
   a. Big sign.
   b. Broken-down car.
   c. Standard-sized cow.
   d. Large fence.

2000

help: *Briggs,* then *size*

This Broadway building was at the corner of Colorado and Los Robles. This view is looking east along Colorado.
circa 1970

*ppl_3451*

317. Thomas W. Ames was having a dispute with his neighbors. After studying the local land use ordinances on the subject, to annoy neighbor Arlene Kraft, he decided it was legal for him to have what placed on his lawn at 619 Woodlyn Road in 1953?
   a. A big sign.
   b. A broken down-car.
   c. A standard-sized cow.
   d. A large fence.

**1950**

help: *Ames, Thom* then *kraft*

318. I killed more than two hundred cattle in Lamanda Park in 1924.
   Because of me you could not take a trip on the Mount Lowe Railway
   I even interfered with the operation of the city incinerator
   What disease am I?
Answer: _____

help: *Lamanda park* then *cattle*

319. As reported in the *Pasadena Star-News*, how many Pasadenans received the Bronze Star in the Vietnamese War?
   a. 2.
   b. 20.
   c. 200.
   d. 2000.

help: *Vietnamese* then *Bronze Star*

*Pasadena. Tournament of Roses. 1902. Girls from Throop Polytechnic Institute entry (taken on steps of school.) Troop Polytechnic was renamed California Institute of Technology in 1920.*

*ppl_8813*

320. The IRS challenged the tax-exempt status of which church because of its anti-war sermons during the war in Iraq in 2005-2006?
 a. All Saints Episcopal Church.
 b. First Baptist Church.
 c. Lake Avenue Congregational Church.
 d. Neighborhood Church.

**2000**

help: *Iraq* then *IRS*


321. In March 2003, protest against the war in Iraq turned ugly where in Pasadena?
 a. Pasadena City College.
 b. Paseo Colorado.
 c. South Lake Avenue.
 d. Throop Unitarian Church.

**2000**

help: *Iraq* then *ugly*


322. In 2006, the Marines honored James Blecksmith, who died in Iraq, by
 a. Building a monument.
 b. Establishing a memorial fund.
 c. Planting some trees.
 d. Renaming a hall.

**2000**

help: *blecksmith*


323. In 2010, Julie Townsend and other members of her Girl Scout team made something that got national recognition. It was a
 a. Cookie distribution network.
 b. Graphic novel.
 c. Recycling bin.
 d. Robot.

**2010**

help: *Girl Scouts* then *Townsend*

324. While speaking at PCC in 2006, then Senator John Kerry made a "joke" about President Bush's policy towards
   a. Education.
   b. Iraq.
   c. The military.
   d. All the above.
   e. No one is really sure.

**2000**

help: Limit by date to 2006, then *kerry, john*


325. Money raised in part by the public paid for what ceremony for Dion Whitley, a graduate from John Muir High School, in 2005?
   a. His burial.
   b. His graduation.
   c. His marriage.
   d. His ordination.

**2000**

help: *whitley, Dion* then *raised*


326. A bit prematurely, perhaps, but what were City Manager C. Wellington Koiner and the Police Chief planning for in August 1944?
   a. Coordinating the return of police officers who had joined the military with those who had replaced them.
   b. Defusing racial tensions when the Japanese who had been interned returned to Pasadena.
   c. Handling celebrations when the war ended in victory.
   d. Planning for parking in the neighborhoods of Linda Vista with the resumption of the games in the Rose Bowl.

**1940**

help: Limit by date to August 1944, then *Koiner*

327. Paul H. Becker, Jr., Caltech student, died in 1939
   a. When his Caltech lab blew up.
   b. When his Caltech "Senior Day Prank" when awry.
   c. When he fell off a cliff on a Caltech field trip.
   d. While playing football for the Caltech football team.

**1930**

help: *Becker, Fred h*


328. Shortly after the end of WWII, sailors from the USS Pasadena found and gave to the city something that was displayed for a time at city hall. It was later returned to Japan in 1955. What was it?
   a. A bell.
   b. A cannon.
   c. A flag.
   d. A scroll.

**1940 1950**

help: *Pasadena (ship)* then *Japan*


329. In 1938, 19 football games were played in the Rose Bowl. For the 1939 football season, how many games were scheduled there?
   a. 11.
   b. 17.
   c. 25.
   d. 32.

**1930**

help: *Rose Bowl, 1939* then *19*

*Because this photo shows a completed Rose Bowl, it was taken after 1928 when the open-ended horseshoe oval was enclosed.*

*ppl_8199*

330. As of August 1948, which professional football team had not yet played in Pasadena?
   a. The Akron Pros.
   b. The Los Angeles Dons.
   c. The New York Yankees.
   d. The San Francisco 49ers.

**1940**

help: Limit date to end with August 1948, then *football team* Then scan the results list.

331. What do USC and Yale have in common in regard to the Rose Bowl game between the years 1915 and 1930?
   a. Both won a Rose Bowl game.
   b. Both lost a Rose Bowl game.
   c. Both turned down an invitation to play in a Rose Bowl game.
   d. Both tied a Rose Bowl game.

help: Limit by date from 1915 to 1930, then *of roses* then *Yale* then *USC*

332. In 2000, director Tim Burton claimed that Pasadena resident David Patrick Bontempo stole 48 of his
   a. Art pieces.
   b. Automobiles.
   c. Cameras.
   d. Ideas.

**2000**

help: *Bontempo,* then *48*

*Designed by William L. Pereira and Charles Luckman, the two-tier, 175,000 square feet J.W. Robinson's Department Store opened May 12, 1958. After closing in January, 1993, Target Stores acquired the property and reopened it in May, 1994.*

*ppl_3427*

333. The cannon (artillery) at Caltech has never been fired in anger. What war was it meant to have been used in?
   a. The Spanish-American War (1898).
   b. The Punitive Expedition in Mexico (1916-1917).
   c. World War One (1914-1918).
   d. United States occupation of Haiti (1915-1934).

help: *artillery* then *fired in anger*


334. John Neil Patterson fought as a pilot in WWI and participated in the 1908 Olympics as a hurdler. With this as a background, he pioneered in the development of
   a. Airports.
   b. Parks.
   c. Roads.
   d. Sanitation.

help: *Patterson, John Neil* then *pioneered*


335. What mystery was revealed in July 1944 involving South Lake Avenue?
   a. What was buried there.
   b. What was going to be built there.
   c. What was going to be torn down there.
   d. Who was buried there.

**1940**

help: Limit by date to July 1944 then *Lake Avenue, South*


336. Welton Becket designed the LA Music Center and which Pasadena department store?
   a. Bullocks on Lake (now Macy's).
   b. Fedco on Colorado (now Target).
   c. Robinson's on Colorado (now Target).
   d. Broadway on Colorado (now not there).

help: *Becket* then *music center*

337. Ten years after opening in 1947, they got permission from the city to spend $1,200,000 on what at Bullock's Pasadena on Lake? (Now it's a Macys.)
   a. Adequate parking.
   c. Big signs.
   c. Decent restaurants.
   d. Diversity training.

**1940**

help: Search by phrase *1,200,000*

338. In 1965, the Pasadena City Council drew the line the third time the Broadway department store that used to be at the corner of Los Robles and Colorado requested that the city do what at Christmas time?
   a. Allow them to expand their hours.
   b. Give them permission to put up a tent.
   c. Provide for extra traffic police.
   d. Supply extra "Super-Sized" dumpsters.

**1960**

help: *Broadway department* then *third*

339. Thomas Bowman disappeared in 1957 when he was 11. When was the case solved?
   a. 1957.
   b. 1977.
   c. 1997.
   d. 2007.

**1950**

help: *Bowman, Thomas* then *solved*

340. Harry R. Kersten, airplane inventor, was named in an arrest warrant in 1942 for which crime?
   a. Arson.
   b. Bigamy.
   c. Burglary.
   d. Embezzlement.

**1940**

help: *Kersten* then *arrest*


341. (Fill in the blank.) In 1925, his _____ had the Red Cross looking for Joseph Edward Grills of Duvall, Washington
   a. Boss.
   b. Daughter.
   b. Parole officer.
   d. Wife.

**1920**

help: *Grills,*


342. In 1924, the day after she was reported missing, Isabel Chavez was found to be in a state of
   a. Bemused befuddlement.
   b. Drunken stupor.
   c. Rigor mortis.
   d. Wedded bliss.

**1920**

help: *Chavez, Is*


343. In 1922, the body of Martin Telles, a 17 year-old Mexican, was found near what?
   a. The Central Library.
   b. The Huntington Hotel.
   c. The power plant.
   d. The Rose Bowl.

**1920**

help: *Telles, Mar*

344. In the 1970's, Harrison H. Schmitt came to Caltech from outer ___?
   a. Banks.
   b. Limits.
   c. Space.
   d. Mongolia.

**1970**

help: *Schmitt, harrison*


345. In 1914, the City was looking for "well-balanced workers" to do what?
   a. Censor objectionable movies.
   b. Check out books.
   c. Hand out parking tickets.
   d. Serve on juries.

**1910**

help: Search by phrase *well-balanced workers*


346. UCLA beat California Institute of Technology in a "Fast Game" of basketball in 1945. The final score was
   a. 29-28.
   b. 39-28.
   c. 49-28.
   d. 109-28.

**1940**

help: *of technology* then *fast game*


347. The Denver Pigs came to Pasadena in 1934 to
   a. Perform at a rodeo.
   b. Peeve suffragists.
   c. Play basketball.
   d. Provide farm-fresh bacon.

**1930**

help: Search by phrase *Denver pigs*

348. In 1894, the Pyke Opera Company presented what comic opera in Pasadena?
   a. H.M.S Pinafore.
   b. Patience.
   c. Princess Ida.
   d. The Mikado.

**1890**

help: *Pyke Opera*


349. In 1916, Miss Grace Adele Pierce did the first something in Pasadena while she
   a. Sang in the shower.
   b. Sat by the Arroyo.
   c. Swallowed her pride.
   d. Swung at a golf ball.

**1910**

help: *Pierce, Grace*


350. Learn to make a tasty cookie,
   Or train your dog named Rex.
   Or get a job even if you are a rookie,
   (And shhh, here are the books some people think should be rated X.)
Where am I?
   a. 1st floor of the Central Library.
   b. 2nd floor of the Central Library.
   c. 3rd floor of the Central Library.
   d. 4th floor of the Central Library.

help: go to the library catalogue http://catalog.pasadenapubliclibrary.net/ipac20/ipac.jsp?profile= and look for books on dog training

351. Mary Ballhorn's dog had a microchip. That proved to be a good thing in 2003 when the dog was found in
    a. Colorado.
    b. Glendale.
    c. Palm Springs.
    d. Tawian.

**2000**

help: *Dogs* then *ball*


352. From March 23-April 4, 2004, Ann Clary Judy was having "family issues" when she ran away and hid in
    a. A friend's house.
    b. Plain sight.
    c. The boiler room.
    d. The closet.

**2000**

help: *Judy, Ann*


353. Mrs. George H. Martin's vision in 1921 was for a Pasadena
    a. Buried in Thin Mints.
    b. Covered with trees.
    c. Enveloped in clean air.
    d. Shielded from Asians.

**1920**

help: *Martin, Mrs. G*


354. While Timothy M. Winders was a Marine serving in Vietnam in 1968, what did he do to win an award from the Girl Scouts?
    a. Bought a lot of cookies.
    b. Helped his sister win a merit badge.
    c. Recommended a rest home to visit.
    d. Wrote a letter.

**1960**

help: *Winders, Tim*

355. In 1914, the Pasadena Day Nursery kept children "safe and amused" while their mothers
   a. Gossiped.
   b. Shopped.
   c. Took classes.
   d. Worked.

**1910**

help: *Pasadena day nu* then *safe and amu*


356. In 1995, which organization celebrated 25 years at Caltech?
   a. Caltech Folk Music Society.
   b. Caltech Israeli Folk Dancing Society.
   c. Caltech Glee Club.
   d. Caltech Gnome Club.

**1990**

help: Limit by date to 1995, then *of technol* then *25 years*


357. In 2005, which organization celebrated "90 years of community building" at Caltech?
   a. Caltech Ballroom Dancing Club.
   b. Caltech Biotech Club.
   c. Caltech Shotokan Karate Club.
   d. Caltech Women's Club.

**2000**

help: Limit by date to 2005 then *of techno* then *90 years*


358. If you were looking for what went missing from Huntington Memorial Hospital in 2002, you would have most reasonably used what to find it?
   a. A dog.
   b. A Geiger counter.
   c. A librarian.
   d. A police officer.

**2000**

help: *Huntington mem* then *missing*

359. John Puckett was killed sometime during World War Two (1939-1945). He was buried in 2005. What item, normally present, caused the funeral to be dealyed?
    a. Missing body.
    b. Missing family.
    c. Missing grave space.
    c. Missing paperwork.

help: *Puckett, Joh*


360. Which of the following was NOT a profession of Albert Clark Reed, Caltech scientist?
    a. Horse groom for Santa Anita.
    b. Flew airplanes for Douglas and Boeing.
    c. Scientist for Project Vista.
    d. Spy for Russia.

help: *Reed, Albert Clark*


361. In addition to being an architectural marvel, the Gamble House has performed shows in 2010 as a
    a. Guerilla theater collective.
    b. Mime troop.
    c. Musical group.
    d. Race horse.

help: *Gamble ho* then *shows*

*David B. Gamble House (Pasadena, Calif.)*

*ppl_4026*

362. In 1914, the Chief of Police complained that there was too much of a certain kind of complaint for the police force to handle, and that someone else should handle it. The type of complaint was
   a. Angry dogs.
   b. Dirty movies.
   c. Prolific litterbugs.
   d. Naughty children.

**1910**

help: Search by phrase *chief of police* then *too much*


363. When Rita McBride became Head of School at Mayfield Senior School in 2002, she wanted her students to
   a. Access.
   b. Excel.
   c. Party.
   d. Sustain.

**2000**

help: *McBride, Rita* then *her students*


364. In 2002, Sequoyah School and New Horizon School combined to create a play about which event?
   a. Airplanes flying into the World Trade Center.
   b. Benjamin Wilson selling land to Hoosiers.
   c. George Washington chopping down a cherry tree.
   d. Spaniards establishing the San Gabriel Mission.

**2000**

help: *Sequoyah* then *new hor*


365. I rode horses in war. (I was in the Army.)
   I rode an Arabian to lead the 1931 Rose Parade. (I didn't like the car.)
   They named a park after me where horses walk through (in Altadena.)
   What is my last name?
   Answer: _____

**1930**

help: *of Roses, 1931* then *Park*

366. Dr. Scherer, president of Caltech, resigned in 1920 because
   a. He didn't like the name change from Throop Polytechnic Institute to California Institute of Technology.
   b. He thought tuition rates were rising too fast.
   c. He wanted to write movies.
   d. Mrs. Scherer suggested, gently, that it was time for him to spend more time with his family.

help: Limit by date to 1920, then *Scherer* then *resigns*


367. After Caltech student Douglas C. Mackenzie beat six hundred other men in 1921, he could have been called a master what?
   a. Magician.
   b. Martial artist.
   c. Marksman.
   d. Mathematician.

help: *Mackenzie, D* then *six hundred*


368. After he beat 600 men at something very manly, what job did Douglas C. MacKenzie go on to do with the Municipality of Pasadena?
   a. Chief of Police.
   b. City Attorney.
   c. City Engineer.
   d. Fire Chief.

help: *Mackenzie, D* then *municipal*

369. In 1935, what was to have stopped the practice of hazing at California Institute of Technology?
   a. A fence.
   b. A fine of $16 (worth $268 in 2013 dollars).
   c. Loss of lab privileges.
   d. Stricter definitions of hazing.

**1930**

help: *of technology* then *hazing*


370. Pasadena police officer Fred Ludlow was going 137 miles per hour in 1938 when he
   a. Caught a bank robber going 124 miles per hour.
   b. Jumped out of a plane with a parachute.
   c. Set a world speed record on a motorcycle.
   d. Was trying to impress the future Mrs. Ludlow.

**1930**

help: *Ludlow, Fred*


371. In 1927, the Pasadena City Council said the City Board of Review had exceeded its authority by banning all the films of
   a. Charlie Chaplin.
   b. Fatty Arbuckle.
   c. Mabel Norman.
   c. Marion Davies.

**1920**

help: *board of review* then *exceeded*


372. George E. "Eddie" Barnhart, veteran of WWI, invented the Wampus-Kat. The Wampus-Kat was
   a. An airplane.
   b. An automobile.
   c. A locomotive.
   d. A scooter.

help: *wampus*

373. According to reports in *Pasadena Star-News*, Kenneth Bell did what in his airplane two days before he died
    a. Shot at Germans.
    b. Set a record for highest altitude.
    c. Set a record for highest air speed.
    d. Set a record for longest time in the air.

help: *Bell, Kenneth*


374. According to reports in the *Los Angeles Times*, Archibald Hoxsey did what in his airplane one day before he died
    a. Shot at Germans.
    b. Set a record for highest altitude.
    c. Set a record for highest air speed.
    d. Set a record longest time in the air.

help: *Hoxsey, A*


375. Theodore Roosevelt told whose mother after her pilot son's death that, "If there were more like him we would have a better country"?
    a. Archibald Hoxsey.
    b. Kenneth Bell.
    c. Leigh Jackson.

help: Search by phrase *if there were more*


376. Between 2007 and 2011, which motion picture has not been seen at Caltech?
    a. "Philosopher Kings."
    b. "An Inconvenient Truth."
    c. "Roachmobile."
    d. "Silent Surrealism."

help: Limit by dates from 2007 to 2011, then *of technology* then *motion picture* then scan the list.

377. How many men have had their arrest for hacking computers at Jet Propulsion Laboratory covered in the newspapers?
    a. 0.
    b. 2.
    c. 4.
    d. 8.

help: *Jet Pro* then *hacking* then count


378. Many people have been arrested for hacking computers at JPL, two of which have come from the same country. The country is
    a. China.
    b. North Korea.
    c. Romania.
    d. Russia.

help: *jet pro* then *hacking* then count


379. Starting in 1921, where was there a "theater in miniature" for the City Board of Review to censor films?
    a. Academy Theater.
    b. Clune's Theater.
    c. Raymond Theater.
    d. Strand Theater.

help: Search by phrase *theater in minia*

*Jet Propulsion Laboratory*
          *ppl_8322*

380. Pasadena High School claimed its first state high school football championship by beating Santa Ana in
   a. 1893.
   b. 1905.
   c. 1915.
   d. 1917.

help: Limit by date from 1893 to 1917, then *Pasadena High School* then *Santa ana*

381. George Barnhart sued the U. S. Government because he rather foolishly gave the government some of the rights to his inventions for the duration of World War Two without talking with a lawyer. Some would say that justice was served after an act of Congress saying in effect that the war was over was signed by President Kennedy in 1962. Later in 1962, Mr. Barnhart
   a. Died, but was $10 million richer before he died.
   b. Died, but was still owed $10 million.
   c. Decided he didn't want the money after all.
   d. Got his money and lived for many more years.

help: *barnhart* then *justice*

382. $10,000,000 in 1962 would be worth about how much in 2013?
   a. $36,700,000
   b. $76,700,000.
   c. $367,000,000
   d. $767,000,000

help: Google *current value of a dollar*, then convert at a web site like measuringworth.com/uscompare

383. (Fill in the blank from this 1949 headline.) "_____ asks use of old hospital."
   a. Librarian.
   b. Mechanic.
   c. Mortician.
   d. Veterinarian.

**1940**

help: Search by phrase *asks use of old*


384. The former unused Isolation Hospital was also made available by the City Council in 1945 as a site for
   a. Day care.
   b. Equipment storage.
   c. Housing.
   d. Vocational education.

**1940**

help: *isolation hospital* then *unused*


385. In September 1910, they put down new what at the polo field at Tournament Park to keep down the "dust evil?"
   a. Gravel.
   b. Oil.
   c. Sod.
   d. Wood chips.

**1910**

help: *Tournament Park* then *dust evil*


386. In September 1910, what kind of races that attracted six thousand persons were run at Tournament Park?
a. Automobile.
b. Chariot.
c. Dog.
d. Motorcycle.

**1910**

help: Limit by date to September 1910 then *Tournament Park* then *races*

387. In 1910, the little zoo at Central Park was described as a
   a. Eden.
   b Eyesore.
   c. Jungle.
   d. Oasis.

**1910**

help: *Central Park* then *little zoo*


388. (Fill in the blank.) When it opened in 1958, Sequoyah School was described by the *Pasadena Star-News* as a new _____ in education?
   a. Challenge.
   b. Experiment.
   c. Tangent.
   d. Trend.

**1950**

help: Set date to 1958, then *Sequoy*


389. Jennifer Thelen was a star volleyball player from Mayfield Senior School in 1996 who was interested in studying what to use what later in life?
   a. A paint brush.
   b. A stethoscope.
   c. A submarine.
   d. A telescope.

**1990**

help: *thelen, J*


390. Fox Field, dedicated in October 1950 at Carmelita Park (now the site of the Norton Simon Museum), was a place where
   a. Children could play.
   b. Dogs could show.
   c. Helicopters could land.
   d. Horses could run.

**1950**

help: Search by phrase *fox field*

391. "Film censorship ends" was an editorial in the *Independent* in what year?
   a. 1961.
   b. 1968.
   c. 1971.
   d. 1978.

help: Limit by artcile type to editorial, then search by phrase *film*


392. In the 1910 *Pasadena Star* headline "Madison girls beat Columbia School six," the six refers to the girls from Columbia School who
   a. Debated topics.
   b. Played basketball.
   c. Performed in a band.
   d. Sewed clothing.

help: Search by phrase *Columbia school six*


393. William McKinley School won a debate against Columbia Grammar School in 1907 assisted by
   a. Silently staring onlookers.
   b. Snappily worn uniforms.
   c. Strategically hidden notes.
   d. Students stridently yelling.

help: *Debates* then *McKinley*


394. If F. N. Finney had had his way in 1910, what would have been the sounds coming from Carmelita Park (now the site of the Norton Simon Museum)?
   a. Airplanes going over a chain-link wall.
   b. Balls going over a wooden wall.
   c. Cars hitting a brick fence.
   d. Dice hitting a cushioned wall.

help: *Finney, F.*

395. In 1910, the city decided to build grandstands at Carmelita Park (now the site of the Norton Simon Museum) so people could see what?
    a. Art.
    b. Football.
    c. Parades.
    d. Tennis.

**1910**

help: *Carmelita* then *grandstands*


396. So rich people could play polo, and despite an appeal by popular minister Robert Burdett, what was removed from 22 acres of Tournament Park in November 1909?
    a. Dogs.
    b. Playing fields.
    c. Poor people.
    d. Trees.

**1900**

help: Search by phrase *22 acres*


397. Unlike some, L. Potter Hitchcock preached from his pulpit at the West Side Congregational Church in 1910, that one ought to
    a. Drink alcohol.
    b. Pay your taxes.
    c. Play cards.
    d. Skip services.

**1910**

help: *Hitchcock, L.*

*Arches in Tournament Park, grown cypress circa 1920*

                    *ppl_13299a*

398. The glow seen over Pasadena in February 1951 was caused by a
   a. Atomic bomb.
   b. Brush fire.
   c. Chemical explosion.
   d. Firework practice.

**1950**

help: Limit by date to 1951, then search by phrase *glow*


399. At the 1909 opening of Carmelita Park as a play facility for children, what sport was not played there?
   a. Baseball.
   b. Basketball.
   c. Football.
   d. Tennis.

**1900**

help: *Carmelita* then *opening*


400. At the 1910 remembering of the opening of Carmelita Park as a play facility for children, what sport was not played there?
   a. Baseball.
   b. Basketball.
   c. Burro polo.
   d. Tennis.

**1910**

help: *Carmelita* then *remem*


401. Sequoyah School celebrated its 45th anniversary in
   a. 1983.
   b. 1993.
   c. 2003.
   d. 2013.

help: *sequo* then *45*

402. A 2009 article in the *Pasadena Journal* touts the focus on what in the kindergarten of Walden School?
 a. Art.
 b. Naps.
 c. Physical education.
 d. Physics.

**2000**

help: *Walden school* then *kinder*


403. In 2000, the Xtreme League decided to have their events at the Coliseum instead of the Rose Bowl. Participants in the Xtreme league
 a. Flew hang gliders.
 b. Performed art.
 c. Played football.
 d. Rode skateboards.

**2000**

help: Search by phrase *Xtreme* then *Colis*


404. Olson Terrible Swedes came to Pasadena in 1933 to
 a. Demonstrate Swedish cooking.
 b. Destroy Volkswagens.
 c. Play basketball at the Armory.
 d. Reenact Viking history.

**1930**

help: *terrible Swedes*

*Pasadena. Rose Bowl, Dedication, 1922.*
*ppl_8193*

405. What happened to 15 houses in October 1967 demonstrated that you really shouldn't build houses in Pasadena made from
   a. Adobe.
   b. Hemp.
   c. Ice.
   d. Tires.

**1960**

help: Search by phrase *15* then *houses*


406. In 1996, who sued the University Club for 1 million dollars for slander?
   a. The Director of Affirmative Action for the City of Pasadena.
   b. The Librarian of the City of Pasadena.
   c. The Mayor of Pasadena.
   d. The Police Chief of Pasadena.

**1990**

help: Search by phrase *slander* then *1 million*


407. (Fill in the blank.) A huge _____ plant was proposed to be built in Pasadena in November 1945.
   a. Atomic power.
   b. Automobile manufacturing.
   c. Agricultural products processing.
   d. Art and beauty products distribution.

**1940**

help: search by phrase *huge* then *plant*


408. Dorothy Dell Goff would have been a star in Hollywood except she accepted what from Pasadena surgeon Karl R. Wagner in 1934?
   a. A drink.
   b. A business offer.
   c. A marriage proposal.
   d. A ride.

**1930**

help: *goff, do*

409. A plausible excuse could be made by someone if they did NOT want to dance with Mrs.Tonika Stayduhar Wright IF they were
   a. A dwarf.
   b. A person who had problems with tricky names.
   c. A vampire.
   d. Rhythmically challenged.

help: *Wright, ton*


410. Among the items that were NOT reported stolen from Mrs. W. S. Wright in 1929 were her
   a. Money.
   b. Peaches.
   c. Purses.
   d. Watches.

help: *wright, mrs. w.*


411. What sewage filled building won a preservation award for the Church of Scientology in 2011?
   a. Avon Building.
   b. Braley Building.
   c. Constance Hotel.
   d. Fannie E. Morrison Horticultural Center.

help: *scientology* then *preservation*


412. Dogs have been celebrated for what on Rose Parade floats?
   a. Assisting the blind.
   b. Military service.
   c. Snowboarding.
   d. All of the above.

help: *Floats* then *Dogs*

413. What blemish nearly cost horse loving Princess Cindy Gillette her spot in the 1961 Rose Parade?
    a. Academic.
    b. Hair.
    c. Moral.
    d. Skin.

**1960**

help: *Gillette, cindy*


414. (Fill in the blank.) In 1999, Lynn Spurlock thought her _____ should not make her ineligible to be on the Rose Court.
    a. Child.
    b. Martial status.
    c. School district.
    d. Weight.

**1990**

help: *spurlock*


415. What did a woman first do in a Pasadena courtroom in 1919?
    a. Serve as a juror.
    b. Settle a case.
    c. Speak as an attorney.
    d. Sue the city.

**1910**

help: Limit by date to 1919, then *Courts* then *Women*


416. After she was arrested and jailed by the Nazis in Germany in 1934, Pasadena musician Isobel Lillian Steele later said she planned to do what?
    a. Commit suicide.
    b. Play a concert.
    c. Protest to President Roosevelt.
    d. Testify against her friends.

**1930**

help: *Steele, Isobel*

417. What was the first name of the Black Pasadenan who ran for City Council in 1929?
   a. Clarence.
   b. James.
   c. Martin.
   d. Thomas.

**1920**

help: *Elections, 1929* then *African Americans*


418. When did the American Legion call for Japanese Americans be removed from Pasadena after the attack on Pearl Harbor on December 7, 1941?
   a. December 10, 1941.
   b. January 7, 1942.
   c. January 28, 1942.
   d. February 15, 1942.

**1940**

help: Limit by date from 12/07/1941 to 02/15/1942, then *japanese americans*


419. What did The Horror, Howard Cantonwine and Tarzan White do in Pasadena in 1939?
   a. Promote a movie.
   b. Roller skate.
   c. Sing.
   d. Wrestle.

**1930**

help: Search by phrase *tarzan white*


420. Louise R. Hoocker ran for City Council in 1927 and 1933. In between she was arrested and convicted of which crime?
   a. Parking wherever she wanted.
   b. Perjury.
   c. Possession of alcohol.
   d. Prostitution.

**1920 1930**

help: *Hoocker,* then *crime*

421. From 1906-1922, what animal had NOT been given to or been part of the City of Pasadena municipal zoo located at Central Park?
   a. An alligator.
   b. A bison.
   c. A coyote.
   d. An eagle.

**1900**

help: *Zoos*


422. According to a November 8, 1970, article in the *Pasadena Star-News*, men, in general, support women to do what at the workplace?
   a. Receive equal pay for equal work.
   b. Work in a discrimination-free environment.
   c. Wear pants.
   d. Work.

**1970**

help: Limit by date to 11/08/1970 then *women*


423. For the first Rose Bowl football game in 1902, which is NOT true:
   a. It made a profit of about $500 (worth about $13,500 today).
   b. The game was played at the Rose Bowl.
   c. The Michigan team was described as being in smiles, the Stanford team in crutches.
   d. The Michigan team was not pleased with its travel arrangements with the railroad.

**1900**

help: *of roses, 1902* then *football*

424. For which Rose Parade did the City of Pasadena first send out tweets during the event?
   a. 2003.
   b. 2008.
   c. 2012.
   d. 2013.

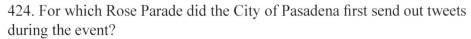

help: *of roses* then *tweets*


425. What is the last name of the Rose Queen who also won a Gold Award (the top award in Girl Scouting)?
Answer: _____

help: *Queen* then *girl scouting*


426. What year did people think there were too many helicopters at the Rose Parade?
   a. 1968.
   b. 1978.
   c. 1998.
   d. 2008.

help: *of Roses* then *helicopters*


427. What did Carrie Humphries and Ron Simms do for the first time on a Rose Parade float in the 1989 parade (in addition to smile and wave)?
   a. Dance.
   b. Dive.
   c. Marry.
   d. Skateboard.

help: *Simms, Ron*

428. Pasadena's team in the Southern California Baseball League did not exist long enough to get a name. How long did they stay in Pasadena before leaving for Santa Barbara in 1913?
   a. 6 hours.
   b. 6 days.
   c. 6 weeks.
   d. 6 months.

**1910**

help: *Southern California Baseball*


429. In 1896, one of the first baseball teams to form in Pasadena was the Pasadena Stars. Other than playing with absurdly small gloves, what else is notable about them?
   a. They worked for the Raymond Hotel.
   b. They were African Americans.
   c. They were Japanese Americans.
   d. They were Mexican Americans.

**1890**

help: Limit by date to 1896, then *Pasadena Stars (Baseball team)*


430. Princess Thea Corcoran of the 1959 Rose Court dreamed of being the next:
   a. Margaret Chase Smith.
   b. Margaret Sanger.
   c. Marie Curie.
   d. Melvil Dewey.

**1950**

sub: *Corcoran, t*

DETAIL OF HIGH SCHOOL FLOAT. THE ARTS

*Scan taken from the article "The Tournament of Roses and Men Who Have Made It" which appeared in California Southland, February / March 1920, pg. 11.*

ppl_10731

431. In 1949 the city cleaned up how many tons of paper after the Rose Parade?
   a. .28 tons (560 pounds, or about the amount of poop produced by an Asian elephant each week).
   b. 2.8 tons (5,600 pounds, or about the weight of an average female Asian elephant).
   c. 28 tons (56,000 pounds, or about the weight of a F/A-18 Hornet airplane).
   d. 280 tons (560,000 pounds, or about the weight of the Caterpillar 797, the worlds largest truck, when empty).

**1940**

help: *Of Roses, 1949* then *tons of paper*


432. Between June 5, 1941, and 1946, Jackie Robinson played for (or at least signed with) many sports teams. During that time what team did he NOT associate with?
   a. The Bears.
   b. The Bruins.
   c. The Bulldogs.
   d. The Red Devils.

**1940**

help: Limit by date from 6/5/1941 to 12/31/1946, then *Robinson, jackie;* then *team*


433. For the 1953 World Series against the New York Yankees, Jackie Robinson was warned against what coming from the Yankee Stadium fans?
   a. Cigarette smoke.
   b. Peanuts.
   c. Profanity.
   d. The Bronx Cheer.

**1950**

help: Limit by date to 1953, then *Robinson, jackie*

434. Royal visitors (nobility) have often participated the Rose Parade. Nobility from which county has NOT been part of the annual parade?
   a. England.
   b. Japan.
   c. Spain.
   d. Thailand.

help: *of Roses* then *royal Visitors*


435. In April 1920, the Pasadena Merchants (baseball team) played a game at Carmelita Park. What was noteworthy about the opposing first baseman?
   a. The number of errors made (0).
   b. The number of fielding plays made (12).
   c. Her first name was Rose.
   d. All of the above.

**1920**

help: Limit by date to april 1920, then *Pasadena Merchants*


436. When the Flagstaff Memorial at the corner of Colorado and Orange Grove was dedicated in 1927 to commemorate Pasadena's participation in World War One, it was estimated that how many men from Pasadena participated in the War?
   a. 24.
   b. 240.
   c. 2400.
   d. 24000.

**1910**

help: *1914-1918* then *flagstaff memorial*

The Goodhue Flagpole, or the Pasadena Memorial Flagpole, was dedicated in 1927.
ppl_8490

437. When the Flagstaff Memorial at the corner of Colorado and Orange Grove was dedicated in 1927 to commemorate Pasadena's participation in World War One, it was estimated that how many women from Pasadena participated in the War?
    a. 4.
    b. 46.
    c. 460.
    d. 4600.

help: *1914-1918* then *flagstaff memorial*


438. In 1924, the city's war record for World War One was completed by a committee headed by Geo. Whittlesey. How many Pasadenans did they say had died in the war?
    a. 4.
    b. 45.
    c. 450.
    d. 4500.

help: *1914-1918* then *war record*


439. Night football at the Rose Bowl were the first West Coast games to be broadcast over a nationwide radio hookup in 1929. Years earlier, what school had their football game played as the first live broadcast of an athletic event?
    a. Caltech.
    b. Occidental.
    c. Pasadena Junior College.
    d. UCLA.

help: *Bowl, 1929* then *radio*

440. I was a soldier in World War Two,
   I quit professional baseball to be an actor,
   I went to the Pasadena Playhouse, and was a doctor on General Hospital.
   What is my last name?
   Answer: _____

help: *baseball* then *playhouse*


441. In what year did the Women's Christian Temperance Union try to make it illegal to smoke on street cars in Pasadena?
   a. 1901.
   b. 1911.
   c. 1921.
   d. 1931.

help: *Temperance Union* then *street*


442. In 1925, the Womens Christian Temperance Union urged the City Council to prohibit the
   a. Drinking of alcohol in theaters.
   b. Drinking of alcohol on street cars.
   c. Smoking of cigarettes in theaters.
   d. Smoking cigarettes on street cars.

**1920**
help: *temperance* then *city council*

443. In 1926, the Women's Christian Temperance Union worked through the City Council to prohibit what?
   a. Percentage billiards (where women were paid 5 cents to play a round of billiards with anyone).
   b. Percentage dancing (where women were paid 5 cents to dance with anyone).
   c. Percentage drinking (where women were paid 25 cents to drink with anyone).
   d. Perentage singing (where women were paid 10¢ to sing to anyone).

**1920**

help: *temperance* then *percentage*


444. In 1906, the Womens Christian Temperance Union urged protection from what on the Fourth of July for street car employees?
   a. Excessive celebrations.
   b. Juvenile delinquency.
   c. Loud fireworks.
   d. Public drunkenness.

**1900**

help: *temperance* then *fourth*


445. In 1963, Lake Avenue Congregational Church broadcast its Sunday sermons over which radio station?
   a. KHJ.
   b. KPCC.
   c. KPSN.
   d. KRLA.

**1960**

help: *congregational* then *radio*

446. In 1906, Sunday School at the Lake Avenue Congregational Church had a
   a. Brotherhood Bureau.
   b. Peace Bureau.
   c. Spirit Bureau.
   d. Travel Bureau.

**1900**

help: *Congregational* then *bureau*


447. In 1897 Pasadena Mayor Calvin Hartwell decided he was going to leave town in a group of seven men to get rich. He believed his fortune was to be won in
   a. Alabama.
   b. Alaska.
   c. Altadena.
   d. Australia.

**1890**

help: *Hartwell* then *seven men*


448. The first time there was a lesson on Islam at Lake Avenue Congregational Church was in
   a. 1917.
   b. 1947.
   c. 1977.
   d. 2007.

help: *congregational* then *islam*


449. Edward J. Taylor came back from the Spanish American War (1898) and became a
   a. Fireman.
   b. Lawyer.
   c. Policeman.
   d. Real estate agent.

**1890**

help: *taylor, edward*

450. The Pasadena chapter of the American Red Cross was organized to
   a. Send materials to hospitals to aid veterans of the Civil War (1861-1865).
   b. Send materials to hospitals during the Spanish American War (1898).
   c. Send aid to victims of the San Francisco Earthquake (1906).
   d. Send materials to hospitals during World War One (1914-1918).

help: *red cross* then *organized*


451. For the Spanish American War (1898), the African-American community formed Troop D. Troop D was known for its use of
   a. Bibles.
   b. Hammers.
   c. Horses.
   d. Spoons.

help: *1898* then *troop d*


452. Following Pancho Villa's raid on Columbus, New Mexico, on March 9, 1916, Company I of the Pasadena National Guard took part in the punitive expedition into Mexico that followed. How many Pasadenans died participating in that raid?
   a. 0.
   b. 1.
   c. 2.
   d. 4.

help: Limit by article type to obituary then *into mexico*

453. Following Pancho Villa's raid on Columbus, New Mexico, on March 9, 1916, Company I of the Pasadena National Guard took part in the punitive expedition into Mexico that followed. After two months in Mexico, what were the troops complaining about?
    a. Lack of action.
    b. Lack of food.
    c. Lack of pay.
    d. Lack of sleep.

**1910**

help: *into mexico* then *two months*


454. After serving as mayor of Pasadena from 1905-1907, William Waterhouse went to Japan as a missionary in 1921. Which was his church here in Pasadena?
    a. First Methodist Church.
    b. Lake Avenue Congregational Church.
    c. Pasadena Presbyterian Church.
    d. Trinity Lutheran Church.

**1900**

help: *waterhouse* then *japan*


455. In April 1942, R. D. Toltschin quit his job working for the city and entered the Army as a pilot. What had been his job with the city?
    a. Accountant.
    b. Engineer.
    c. Janitor.
    d. Policeman.

**1940**

help: *Toltsch*

456. In April 1942, 120 was the number of what?
   a. Automobile tires that could be sold.
   b. Japanese families relocated out of the city.
   c. People cited for breaking the blackout regulations.
   d. Students caught ditching school.

**1940**

help: Limit search by date to April 1942, then search by phrase *142*


457. Edgar C. Outten was described as the Poet Laureate of City Hall in 1942. When not writing poetry, what was his day job?
   a. An accountant.
   b. A janitor.
   c. A librarian.
   d. A policeman.

**1940**

help: Search by phrase *poet laur*


458. In 1911, the City of Pasadena presented to Adolphus and Lilly Busch (they of Busch Gardens and beer) an elaborate cup to commemorate their 50th wedding anniversary. Which Pasadena institution protested this act?
   a. Lake Avenue Congregational Church.
   b. Orange Grove Meeting of the Society of Friends.
   c. Sons of Saint George.
   d. Womens Christian Temperance Union.

**1910**

help: *Busch, ado* then *protested*

*Mrs. Lillie Busch, widow of Adolphus Busch, who created the great Busch Gardens Veterans' Relief Fund which has brought help to hundreds of disabled ex-service men and women. She placed the administration of the far-famed Busch Gardens in the hands of a committee of American Legion officials, and all the money derived from admission charged is used for the relief of veterans who need immediate aid. Scan from California Life, November 11, 1922, pg. 3.*

*ppl_10827*

459. As a war memorial for World War Two, in 1948 the city was going to have Gordon Kaufmann spend $35,000,000 on what?
   a. An airport.
   b. A fountain/water garden complex.
   c. A library.
   d. An opera house.

**1940**

help: *1945* then *35,000,000*


460. Which Pasadena resident won the Congressional Medal of Honor and had a local Army base (at the Vista del Arroyo) named after him?
   a. Charles Henry Pierce.
   b. Gaines Lawson.
   c. Joe Hayashi.
   d. Raymond Harvey.
   e. Reginald B. Desiderio.

help: *medal of honor* then *vista del*


461. Which Pasadenan won the Congressional Medal of Honor for his service during the Philippine American war?
   a. Charles Henry Pierce.
   b. Gaines Lawson.
   c. Joe Hayashi.
   d. Raymond Harvey.
   e. Reginald B. Desiderio.

help: *medal of honor* then *philippine*

462. Which Pasadenan won the Congressional Medal of Honor for his service during the Korean War, and also served in World War Two?
   a. Charles Henry Pierce.
   b. Gaines Lawson.
   c. Joe Hayashi.
   d. Raymond Harvey.
   e. Reginald B. Desiderio.

**1940 1950**

help: *medal of honor* then *korean war* then scan list


463. What is the first name of the only Japanese American from Pasadena to win the Congressional Medal of Honor for his service during World War Two?
   a. Charles.
   b. Jim.
   c. Joe.
   d. Raymond.

**1940**

help: *medal of honor* then *japanese*


464. In 1947, General Mark Clark nominated Richard J. Barrett for what military award?
a. The Bronze Star.
b. The Congressional Medal of Honor.
c. The Legion of Merit.
d. The Silver Star.

**1940**

help: *barrett, richard*

465. David Abbey Paige got a Congressional Medal for his work with explorer Richard Byrd in 1937. He got the award for his skill with a
 a. Compass.
 b. Gun.
 c. Paintbrush.
 d. Typewriter.

**1930**

help: *paige, David*


466. Some people think results of the 1959 fire at Simpson's Nursery and Pet Store are still with us today in the form of
 a. Cats.
 b. Iguanas.
 c. Mediterranean fruit flies.
 d. Parrots.

**1950**

help: *Nursery and Pet*


467. When the Ku Klux Klan was active in Pasadena around 1925, where was their presence the most controversial?
 a. As members of the Chamber of Commerce.
 b. As members of the police department.
 c. As members of the Tournament of Roses Association.
 d. As members of the YMCA.

**1920**

help: *ku Klux Klan*


468. When did Sarah Ferguson, Duchess of York, first visit Pasadena?
 a. 1990.
 b. 1993.
 c. 1996.
 d. 1999.

**1990** 

help: *ferguson, s* then scroll to bottom of the list

469. With a background in social work, the first woman to be hired by the Pasadena police department was Helen Berry Johnston. She was hired in
   a. 1905.
   b. 1915.
   c. 1925.
   d. 1935.

help: *johnston, helen*


470. Police were halting people with faulty headlights in October 1926 because
   a. Someone had complained A LOT to the City Council.
   b. The city needed the money.
   c. The police chief went to a conference.
   d. Winter was coming; the goose was presumably getting fat.

**1920**

help: *police* then *headlights*


471. In 1927, tear bombs or tear gas were first used by the Pasadena police department to
   a. Attempt to dislodge a demented sniper.
   b. Disperse Pasadena Junior College students having a snowball fight.
   c. Enter and interrupt a Chinese lottery.
   d. Provide inadvertent cover that allowed a bookie suspect to escape.

**1920**

help: *police* then *tear*


472. In the 1928 gunfight between K.W. Petschu (thought to be demented) and Lee R. Culver (of the Pasadena police department), who had the rifle?
   a. K.W. Petschu.
   b. Lee R. Culver.

**1920**

help: *Petschu*

473. (Fill in the blank) Pasadena police officer Gairie M. Upshaw was a member of the U. S. _____ team
   a. Fencing.
   b. Tennis.
   c. Wrestling.
   d. Rifle.

help: *upshaw*


474. Why did Pasadena motorcycle police officer Gairie M. Upshaw miss the tryouts for the 1932 national team?
   a. He couldn't get time off work.
   b. He had an accident responding to a call.
   c. He overslept.
   d. He wanted to spend more time with his family.

**1930**

help: *upshaw, gai* then *tryouts*


475. Why did William A. Beal resign from the police department in 1928?
a. To avoid further embarrassment to the department.
b. To go fishing.
c. To join the fire department.
d. To promote his inventions.

**1920**

help: *beal, will*


476. Police officer Robert Emmett O'Rourke was noted for his
   a. Camera eye.
   b. Iron stomach.
   c. Steady hand.
   d. Iron stomach.

help: *rourke, Robert Emm* then *noted*

477. In a 1924 interview for the *Pasadena Evening Post*, police officer Robert Emmett O'Rourke said that the modern criminal was NOT a
    a. Blockhead.
    b. Dumbbell.
    c. Numbskull.
    d. Pudden-head.

**1920**

help: *rourke, Robert Em* then *modern*


478. In 1924, women were placed in charge of what part of police business?
    a. Dealing with children.
    b. Jailors for women.
    c. Handling the phones.
    d. Typing reports.

**1920**

help: Limit by date to 1924, then *women* then *police*


479. According to the local press, the Pasadena police department has only been able to find and stop one wild orgy in Pasadena. With the lure of booze and dancing girls, in what part of town did this party happen in 1924?
    a. Arroyo Seco.
    b. Bungalow Heaven.
    c. Linda Vista.
    d. San Rafael.

**1920**

help: Search by phrase *wild orgy*

480. In what year was the expertise of the Pasadena police department called upon to make air trips safe?
   a. 1921.
   b. 1941.
   c. 1981.
   d. 2001.

help: *police* then *air trips*


481. When found in the company of men gambling during a raid by police in 1921, police officer J. C. Lawrence told his fellow officers that he was there not to gamble, but he
   a. Had no idea it was that kind of place, and he was shocked, shocked to find that gambling was going on in here.
   b. Was serving as an undercover police officer.
   c. Was there as a favor to a friend who needed a ride.
   d. Was there merely as a spectator.

**1920**

help: *Lawrence, J. C.*


482. Vigilantes (whose names were kept secret) were recruited by the police department in Pasadena in the 1920's to deal with what?
   a. Cattle rustling.
   b. Selling alcohol.
   c. Traffic violations.
   d. Unkempt yards.

**1920**

help: Search by phrase *vigilantes*

483. In what might be seen as a misapplication of city resources, in 1924 motorcycle police officers Joe Rodman and Henry Collins were sent to catch a
    a. Cat.
    b. Frog.
    c. Snake.
    d. Turtle.

**1920**

help: *rodman, j*


484. I was a nudist, I was an author,
    With a woman's name I didn't bother.
        My husband had scales,
        And I told my tales.
    Alas! His fame went so much more farther.
What was my last name?

help: Search by phrase *nudist*


485. Busch Gardens served the interests of the United States in two ways in connection with World War One. First, the grounds were confiscated by the federal government, perhaps to have been used as a hospital (the property was actually returned to Mrs. Busch before the property it was destroyed). Second, it was used as a fundraising location for the following organizations to raise money for the war or its veterans:
The American Red Cross: $12,000 in 1918;
The American Legion: $130,000 in 1928.
About how much money was raised on the grounds of Busch Gardens to pay for the costs of World War One in 2013 dollars?
    a. $78,000.
    b. $142,000.
    c. $1,900,000.
    d. $10,160,000.

**1910 1920**

help: Google *current value of a dollar*, then convert each year to 2013 values at a web site like measuringworth.com/uscompare, then add

486. Pasadena has been the name of several ships that have served in various war efforts. In World War One there was the freighter Crown City (sunk 9/1/1942); in World War Two there was the Cruiser USS Pasadena and after the war a nuclear submarine was also named after Pasadena. There was also a Liberty Ship (freighter) that was named after a Pasadena clergyman when it was christened by Mrs. Robert A. Millikan in November, 1942. What was the name of that clergyman?
    a. Amos G. Throop.
    b. Robert Freeman.
    c. Josiah Sibley.
    d. John M. McCarthy.

help: Search by phrase *christened*


487. Richard Edward Garcia, a Hispanic American, was the first Pasadenan reported killed by the U. S. military in December of 1941(after Pearl Harbor). Why were his parents and friends happy to read the *Pasadena Post* January 2, 1942?
    a. He got a medal.
    b. He was captured.
    c. He was alive.
    d. His brother was alive.

help: *Garcia, richard*


488. On January 25, 1941, the *Pasadena Star-News* reported that the first Pasadenan to be killed in World War Two, Anthony Worcester, was fighting for which country?
    a. Canada.
    b. England.
    c. Germany.
    d. United States.

help: *worcester,*

489. Hulett Clinton Merritt, Pasadena millionaire, was convicted of a crime in connection with World War One. Hulett Clinton Merritt, being a Pasadena millionaire, took his conviction up to the United States Supreme Court where it was overturned. What crime was Hulett Clinton Merritt, Pasadena millionaire, initially convicted of?
   a. Driving while drunk.
   b. Evading the draft.
   c. Hoarding food.
   d. Violating the blackout.

**1910**

help: *merritt, hu* then *supreme court*


490. 1950 saw what improvements go up on Colorado Boulevard?
   a. Backs to benches.
   b. Brighter street lights.
   c. Irrigation for trees.
   d. Taller poles for banners.

**1950**

help: *colorado bou* then *go up*


491. What did the city manager and the Pacific Electric Railway Company discuss in June, 1950?
   a. Bringing light railroad to Pasadena.
   b. Bringing more bus lines to Pasadena.
   c. Bus fares on bus lines to Pasadena.
   d. Removing street railroad tracks from Pasadena.

**1950**

help: *pacific electric* then *city manager*

*Taken after 1897. This is when Pasadena Drug Company moved to 65 E. Colorado and when Daggett and Daggett moved to 17 N. Raymond. This photo displays the Northwest corner of the intersection of Raymond and Colorado.*

*ppl_4099*

492. In 1919, the Red Cross sold 8000 what in the interests of public health?
   a. Bandages.
   b. Birth control.
   c. Masks.
   d. Syringes.

1910

help: *Red cross* then *8000*


493. In 1919, a new law made it a crime if a hotel guest did what?
   a. Buy non-licensed Rose Parade merchandise.
   b. Not wear a mask.
   c. Skateboarded on the grounds.
   d. Took his drink outside the dining room.

1910

help: *law* then *hotel guests*


494. In 1918, a servant was told that she could not quit her employer. If she did, she was told, she would be sent to a prison camp for aliens. She was from
   a. Germany.
   b. Italy.
   c. Japan.
   d. Mexico.

1910

help: Search by phrase *servant* then *prison camp*


495. Registration of enemy aliens began on February 4, 1918. A few months later, someone thought of women. Which type of women were expected to register before June 17, 1918?
   a. Austrian-Hungarian women.
   b. German women.
   c. Both German and Austrian-Hungarian women.
   d. Women were not required to register.

1910

help: Search by phrase *expected to register*

496. In 1916, the City Council decided that more regulation was needed in what local industry?
   a. Billiard parlors.
   b. Junk dealers.
   c. Milk producers.
   d. Pushcart vendors.

help: Limit by date to 1916, then *city council* then *regulation*


497. In 1976, the City Council decided that more regulation was needed in the consumption of
   a. Alcohol.
   b. Cigarettes.
   c. Sugar.
   d. Pornography.

help: Limit by date to 1976, then *city Council* then *regulation*


498. In 1915, the police department and the City Attorney had a disagreement about witnesses. The police said you could
   a. Use the testimony of a beaten wife if she declined to press charges.
   b. Use the testimony of a child against a family member.
   c. Use the testimony of a Chinese witness.
   d. Use the testimony of a paid witness.

help: *city attorney* then *witnesses*

499. The first woman officer was appointed to the police department in 1925. The first time that someone wrote in the newspaper anyone wanted women on the force was
   a. 1884.
   b. 1894.
   c. 1914.
   d. 1924.

**1920**

help: *police department* then *wants women*


500. In 1915, the Police Chief McIntyre was looking forward to making what available for policemen?
   a. Higher wages.
   b. More comfortable uniforms.
   c. Overtime.
   d. Pensions.

**1910**

help: Limit by date to 1915, then *police department* then *policemen*


501. In 1914, the chief of police said there were too many complaints about what for his officers to deal with?
a. Censor moving pictures.
b. Enforce alcohol laws.
c. Regulate junk dealers.
d. Track down truant students.

**1910**

help: Search by phrase *chief of police* then *complaints*

502. In 1911, the Pasadena Star reported that Police Sergeant J. O. Reynolds had lost and then spent years looking for what in the mountains?
   a. His dog.
   b. His gold mine.
   c. His one true love (not a dog).
   d. His wedding ring.

**1910**

help: *reynolds, j. o.*


503. To catch all the "auto speeders," when did Pasadena police get their new motorbikes?
   a. 1905.
   b. 1910.
   c. 1915.
   d. 1920.

help: Search by phrase *new motorbikes*


504. Claiming that its presence hurt real estate values, there were bomb threats against which Pasadena entity in 1910?
   a. First African Methodist Episcopal Church.
   b. First Church of the Nazarene.
   c. Pasadena Jewish Temple.
   d. Orange Grove Meeting of the Religious Society of Friends.

**1910**

help: *bomb threats* then *real estate*

505. Basketball great Pete Maravich died at a pickup basketball game at which Pasadena church or temple in 1988?
    a. First African Methodist Episcopal Church.
    b. First Church of the Nazarene.
    c. Pasadena Jewish Temple.
    d. Orange Grove Meeting of the Religious Society of Friends.

**1980**

help: *maravich,*


506. The Peace Through Music program, which has been held at the First Church of the Nazarene with the sponsorship of the Human Relations Commission and its member Nat Nehdar, first marked an event held to heal after
    a. Columbine.
    b. Halloween murders.
    c. 9/11.
    d. Sandy Hook.

help: *peace through* then *first marked*


507. Where did Pasadena's first fully accessible playground for the disabled open in 2007?
    a. All Saints Episcopal Church.
    b. Brookside Park.
    c. First Church of the Nazarene.
    d. La Pintoresca Park .

**2000**

help: Search by phrase *first fully access*

508. The First Church of the Nazarene celebrated its Centennial Celebration with Congressman Adam Schiff in what year?
   a. 2010.
   b. 2005.
   c. 1995.
   d. 1990.

help: *of the naz* then *schiff*


509. In 1942, the majority of the directors of the Shakespeare Club received tickets for what activity? (But the charges were dropped because of a legal loophole.)
   a. Allowing their lawn to become too overgrown.
   b. Consuming alcohol in a club without a liquor license.
   c. Honking their car horns too loud on Shakespeare's birthday.
   d. Parking overtime on city streets.

help: *shakespeare club* then *loophole*


510. What is the last name of the John Muir Alumni who has been both a Rose Princess and an Olympian?
Answer:_____

help: *Olympics,* then *Princesses*


511. In 1942, Caltech student Jack Warren won a contest winner for his skill at what?
   a. Doing math in his head.
   b. Dressing as a girl.
   c. Playing chess.
   d. Taking care of lab animals.

help: *warren, jack*

512. In 1932, an article in the *Pasadena Star-News* interviewed the type of women Caltech men would marry. Judging by the headline, which virtue did the men of Caltech most look for in a wife?
   a. Compatible personality.
   b. Homely virtues.
   c. Intelligence.
   d. Motherhood.

**1930**

help: Limit by date to 1932, then *of tech* then *women*


513. In 1942, three neighbors in the Linda Vista neighborhood joined together
   a. To assist neighbors in brush clearance.
   b. To complain about the lack of a local library.
   c. To protest excessive use of the Rose Bowl.
   d. To start a community garden.

**1940**

help: *linda vista* then *three neigh*


514. While in office for one term (1991-1995), African American City Councilman Isaac Richard publicly feuded with
   a. Chris Holden.
   b. Rick Cole.
   c. Phyliss Mueller.
   d. The Annandale Golf Course.
   e. The Brookside Golf Course.
   f. The entire Pasadena City Council (except himself).
   g. The Northwest Commission.
   h. The Pasadena Community Health Center.
   i. The Pasadena Police Department.
   j. The Rose Bowl Aquatic Center.
   k. The Rose Bowl Operating Company.
   l. The Tournament of Roses Association.
   m. The World Cup.
   n. All of the above.

**1990**

help: *richard, isaa*

515. For a hole-in-one at Brookside Golf Course in 1985, Pat Cabot got a
   a. Free dinner.
   b. Pat on the back.
   c. Toyota automobile.
   d. Year of free golf.

**1980**

help: Search by phrase *hole-in-one*


516. Andrew Carnegie's greatest gift to Pasadena was given in 1919. Was it a
   a. Golf course.
   b. Library.
   c. Observatory.
   d. School.

**1910**

help: *carnegie, and* then *gift*


517. The same week in 1906 that contractors filed the contracts on Howard Huntington's house, which other Pasadena institution filed construction plans?
   a. Annandale Golf Club.
   b. First Christian Church.
   c. James A. Garfield Elementary School.
   d. Throop Polytechnic Institute.

**1900**

help: Search by phrase *howard hunt* then *contract*


518. In 1892, tomato cans were used as
   a. Holes in golf courses.
   b. Mitts for baseball games.
   c. Patches on car mufflers.
   d. Traps for mice.

**1890** 📶

help: Search by phrase *tomato cans*

519. (Fill in the blank.) Lured with the promise of Pasadena water, the area around Annandale Golf Club voted to be annexed to Pasadena in 1917. The number of people who voted yes was greater than the number who voted no by _____ ?
a. 1.
b. 10.
c. 100.
d. 1000.

**1910**

help: *annandale golf* then *annex*


520. Jin McHale was picked as the nation's leading amateur what in 1936?
   a. Dancer.
   b. Diver.
   c. Golfer.
   d. Tennis player.

**1930**

help: search by phrase *leading ama*


521. (Fill in the blank.) A missionary, Emma E. Dickinson, died and left $45,000 and some curios to the city in 1926. The curios seem to have been misplaced, but the money was used to build a _____ in the Arroyo Seco in the 1930's.
   a. Archery range.
   b. Bird bath.
   c. Casting pond.
   d. Horse trail.

**1930**

help: *dickinson,* then *arroyo*

522. In 1914, Maurice Walton got paid $1,000 (worth about $23,700 in 2013 dollars) to demonstrate what at the Huntington Hotel?
    a. Basketball.
    b. Flower arrangement.
    c. Hat design.
    d. Tango dancing.

**1910**

help: *walton, maurice*


523. Mrs. Montgomery Ward and her daughter were delayed by what to the Hotel Green in 1914?
    a. A death in the family.
    b. A fear of roses.
    c. A railroad strike.
    d. A storm.

**1910**

help: *ward, mrs.*


524. Charles J. Fox was picked to be part of the board governing which sport for the 1932 Olympics?
    a. Bicycling.
    b. Lawn bowling.
    c. Rowing.
    d. Weightlifting.

**1930**

help: *fox, ch* then *olympics,*

*Children's Parade by the Green Hotel*

*ppl_655*

525. In 1935, the governor of what saw a performance of "Henry VI" at the Pasadena Playhouse?
   a. Bali.
   b. Burma.
   c. Missouri.
   d. Montana.

**1930**

help: *pasadena play* then *governor*


526. I was a member of the Pasadena City Council
   I was a famous building contractor
   I built the Hotel Green and the First Presbyterian Church
   I named a Block after me
   What is my last name?
   Answer:_____

help: *City Council* then *contractor*


527. In a perhaps misguided attempt to make children feel comfortable when school integration (busing) was implemented, according to a Sept 9, 1970, *Los Angeles Times* article, what item was said to be "too sweet" to be placed on the bus for them?
   a. Bus etiquette guides.
   b. Candy canes.
   c. Copies of the Spangler decision.
   d. Disco balls.

**1970**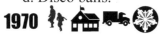

help: *school integration* then *too sweet*

528. Colorado Street was renamed Colorado Boulevard in 1958. In 1932 there was a suggestion that involved re-naming Colorado Street to
    a. Crown City Boulevard.
    b. Hoover Boulevard.
    c. Pasadena Boulevard.
    d. Rose Parade Boulevard.

**1930**

help: Search by phrase *Colorado street* then *re-nam*


529. The Old Mill, or El Molino Viejo, was preserved in 1914 when the Huntington Hotel incorporated it in its grounds as a
    a. Caretaker's cottage.
    b. Golf clubhouse.
    c. Storage shed.
    d. VIP bungalow.

**1910**

help: *el molino viejo* then *huntington*


530. (Fill in the blank.) Wanting to broaden the recreational opportunities for its citizens, in 1930 the City Council voted to allow a new _____ on California Boulevard.
    a. Drive-in movie theater.
    b. Campground.
    c. Miniature golf course.
    d. Spanish language movie theater.

**1930**

help: Limit by date to 1930, then *city council* then *california*

531. In 1929, to go along with the Municipal Golf Course (Brookside Golf Course), it was proposed the city also build what other municipal athletic field?
    a. Baseball.
    b. Horseshoe.
    c. Polo.
    d. Soccer.

**1920**
help: Limit by date to 1929, then *brookside golf* then *field*


532. In 1928, the day the Brookside Golf Course opened, the throng enjoyed a free
    a. Breakfast.
    b. Golf ball.
    c. Parking.
    d. Round of golf.

**1920**
help: *Brookside golf* then *throng*


533. When, according to the *Pasadena Weekly*, did the city get serious about bringing the National Football League to the Rose Bowl?
    a. 1997.
    b. 2002.
    c. 2007.
    d. 2012.

help: Limit by publication to the *Pasadena Weekly*. Then *Rose Bowl*, then *serious*

534. The citizens of Linda Vista have opposed the use of the Rose Bowl by the National Football League as a site for home football games by a professional team at least since
    a. 1997.
    b. 2002.
    c. 2007.
    d. 2012.

help: *Linda vista* then *National Football Lea*


535. In 1924, James W. Reagan proposed that the Rose Bowl be replaced by
    a. An arts center.
    b. A lake.
    c. A parking lot.
    d. Nothing that would never, ever attract visitors, especially if they were to drive and then park there.

**1930**

help: *Reagan* then *rose bowl*


536. Our Lady of Guadalupe Church burned in
    a. 1967.
    b. 1977.
    c. 1987.
    d. 1997.

help: *lupe church* then *fire*

*Originally opened in 1907 as the Hotel Wentworth, it was purchased by Henry Huntington in 1911 and reopened in 1914 as the Huntington Hotel.*

    *ppl_5178*

537. To publicize the play "Happiest Millionaire" in 1958, the Pasadena Playhouse
   a. Had actors dressed as rich people handing out fliers.
   b. Had rich people dressed as actors handing out $5 bills.
   c. Hid $5 bills in public.
   d. Threw free tickets from a balloon.

help: *happiest millionaire*


538. Robert Weston Smith returned to work in 1984 at the Huntington-Sheraton Hotel. He was employed as a
   a. Cook.
   b. Concierge.
   c. Gardener.
   d. Radio disc jockey.

help: *smith, robert w*


539. According to an article written in 1987, what helped launch the Pasadena Playhouse?
   a. Actors.
   b. Cash.
   c. Hugs.
   d. Umbrellas.

help: *pasadena playhouse* then *launch*

540. (Fill in the blank.) When the Pasadena Playhouse filed for bankruptcy in April 2010, it was for the _____ time?
   a. First.
   b. Second.
   c. Third.
   d. Fourth.

**2010**

help: Limit by dates to April 2010, then *playhouse* then *bank*


541. In 1914, Saint Andrew's Church established a separate church to serve which community?
   a. African American.
   b. Armenian.
   c. German.
   d. Hispanic.

**1910**

help: *saint andrew* then *established*


542. Before he was ordained as a priest, in 1951 Kenyon L. Reynolds gained fame while wearing
   a. A gun and a badge.
   b. A pocket protector and a slide rule.
   c. A suit and a tie.
   d. Gym shoes and shorts.

**1950**

help: *Reynolds, ken*

543. How long did it take Carlo Wostry to paint the canvasses at Saint Andrew's Church?
   a. 3 months.
   b. 12 months.
   c. 18 months.
   d. 36 months.

help: *wostry, carlo*


544. Kilroy was Saint Andrew's School first
   a. Graffiti.
   b. Mascot.
   c. Musical.
   d. Teacher.

help: *andrew's school* then *kilroy*


545. (Fill in the blank.) In 1906, the fire department said that Saint Andrew's Church had one of safest _____ in the city.
   a. Baptismal font.
   b. Bell tower.
   c. Entrance.
   d. Evacuation plan.

help: *andrew's church* then *fire depart*


546. A replica of Our Lady of Guadalupe visited Saint Andrew's Church in
   a. 1919.
   b. 1949.
   c. 1979.
   d. 1999.

help: *andrew's church* then *replica*

547. Somewhat improbably perhaps, but according to a letter to the editor by Mary Q. Marino, the thing that made the annual Saint Andrew's Church's fiesta a hit in 1999 were the
   a. Animals.
   b. Beer.
   c. Children.
   d. Fliers.

**1990**

help: Search by author *marino, mary*


548. Having its world premier at the Pasadena Playhouse in 1928, which play by Eugene O'Neill was described as the most significant contribution to modern theatrical history?
   a. "Ah, Wilderness!"
   b. "Lazarus Laughed."
   c. "Long Day's Journey Into Night."
   d. "The Iceman Cometh."

**1920**

help: Limit by article type to performance review, then *o'Neill* then *modern thea*


549. In 1910, the baseball team from Throop Polytechnic Institute, later Caltech, beat Colton 8 to 0. The pitcher for Throop was a "brunette twirler." He was
   a. An African American.
   b. An Armenian American.
   c. A Hispanic American.
   d. A Japanese American.

**1910**

help: *throop poly* then *colton*

550. For a few months in 1909, there was a baseball team composed of Hispanic-Americans called the Esperanza. In February of that year they played a team from what community?
   a. African American.
   b. Armenian.
   c. German.
   d. Japanese.

**1900**

help: *esperanza (base*

551. In 1909, the owner of the Pasadena Pharmacy was cited for selling alcohol illegally. His arrest was facilitated by a special officer (undercover officer) from which community?
   a. African American.
   b. Armenian.
   c. Hispanic.
   d. Japanese.

**1900**

help: *pasadena pharm* then *special office*

552. In an exercise of real-world applied physics at Caltech in 1931, the physics department played the biology department. Who won by two goals?
   a. Biology department.
   b. Physics department.

**1930**

help: *of technol* then *two goals*

553. After losing 49-0 in the 1902 Rose Bowl, in 1917 Stanford offered to play what sport for the Rose Tournament?
   a. Baseball.
   b. Polo.
   c. Soccer.
   d. Water polo.

**1910**

help: *of roses, 1917* then *Stanford*

554. The first reported soccer match in Pasadena happened in what year?
   a. 1914.
   b. 1924.
   c. 1934.
   d. 1944.

help: Limit by dates from 1914 to 1944, then *soccer* then scroll down to the bottom of the list


555. I was one of three to make the national team in soccer
   I later signed a three-year deal with the Galaxy
   My last name is Jones
   What is my first name?
   Answer: _____

help: Search by phrase *National team* then *jones*


556. El Matador from Mexico played for what Pasadena team from 2000-2001?
   a. Beavers.
   b. Galaxy.
   c. Lancers.
   d. Panthers.

**2000**

help: Search by phrase *el matador*


557. "Renew, Re-view, Revive" was the 2001 slogan for which Pasadena organization?
   a. Pasadena Planning Department.
   b. Pasadena Playhouse.
   c. Saint Andrew's Church.
   d. Target Store.

**2000**

help: Search by phrase *renew, re-view*

558. In August 1916, what topic was growing in popularity at the Pasadena Public Library?
   a. Anthropology.
   b. History.
   c. Political science.
   d. Sociology.

**1910**

help: *public library* then *popularity*


559. Which Pasadena church fought the city over taxation (revenue to the city) and freedom of religion in 1961?
   a. All Saints Episcopal Church.
   b. Church of the Brethren.
   c. Lincoln Avenue Methodist Church.
   d. Saint Andrew's Church.

**1960**

help: *of religion* then *revenue*


560. In 1910, the Lake Avenue Methodist Church beat All Saints Episcopal Church at
   a. Basketball.
   b. Checkers.
   c. Indoor baseball.
   d. Pushball.

**1910**

help: *avenue meth* then *all saint*


561. When Pasadena opened a new City Hall in 1903, the liquor in the old City Hall was
   a. Consumed by City Hall employees.
   b. Dumped in the streets around City Hall.
   c. Moved to the new City Hall.
   d. Sold to people hanging around City Hall.

**1900**

help: *city hall* then *liquor*

562. I was a participant in the Iran hostage crisis, 1979-1981
My father was a pastor at First Church of the Nazarene
I was a big Kenny Rogers fan
What is my last name?
Answer: _____

**1970  1980**

help: *of the naz* then *hostage*


563. (Fill in the blank.) According to a 1919 *Pasadena Star-News* editorial, Albert I, King of the Belgians, was _____ when he visited Pasadena.
   a. Charming.
   b. Rude.
   c. Jovial.
   d. Ungracious.

**1910**

help: Limit by artcile type to editorial, then *albert I, King*


564. Who was Helen Hay?
   a. Artist who went to Paris and exhibited.
   b. Missionary who went to China and was interned.
   c. Nurse who went to Russia during World War One and administered.
   d. Writer who went to New York and wrote.

help: *hay, helen*


565. What did Hester F. Cattell do for the first time as a Pasadena woman in 1911?
   a. Argue a case before a jury in public.
   b. Dance as a Grecian nymph in public.
   c. Register to vote in public.
   d. Sing "Alexander's Ragtime Band" in public.

**1910**

help: *cattell, he*

*We suspect this photo was taken during the visit by General Pershing to Pasadena in 1920.*
*ppl_3712*

566. Katherine Hobbs' chief complaint about her housemate Sally Baird from 1981-1982 was that she
   a. Liked jazz.
   b. Had a husband.
   c. Never picked up her clothes.
   d. Was alive.

help: *hobbs, kath* then *baird, sal*


567. Which bank in Pasadena is said to be haunted?
   a. OneWest Bank.
   b. Security Pacific Bank.
   c. Union Savings Bank.
   d. Wells Fargo Bank.

help: *haunted* then *bank*


568. Which number is connected to a court said to be haunted in Pasadena?
   a. 3.
   b. 6.
   c. 9.
   d. 23.

help: *haunted* then *court*


569. Of the eight or so Pasadena geniuses (as defined by receiving an award from the MacArthur Foundation) how many have been noted primarily for being authors?
   a. 0.
   b. 1.
   c. 2.
   d. 3.

help: *macarthur foundation* then *authors*

570. The Fourth of July celebration at the Rose Bowl in 2000 featured a 23-minute fireworks show and
    a. An appearance by President Bill Clinton.
    b. A concert by Garth Brooks.
    c. A demonstration by Cirque du Soleil.
    d. A soccer match by the Galaxy soccer team.

**2000**

help: *fourth of july* then *Rose Bowl, 2000*


571. Although some consider it unlucky to say the name of the play out loud, when did Madame Modjeska (who later died) perform "MacBeth" at the Pasadena Grand Opera House (which was later torn down) in Pasadena?
    a. 1894.
    b. 1904
    c. 1914.
    d. 1924.

help: *macbeth* then *Modjeska*


572. In 1999, the Pasadena Playhouse combined Shakespeare's words from "Twelfth Night" and the music of
    a. Al Jolson.
    b. Duke Ellington.
    c. The Beatles.
    d. The Talking Heads.

**1990**

help: *th night* then *music*

573. What is the last name of the Pasadenan who both was a Rose Queen and Wimbledon champ?
   a. Sutton.
   b. Vines.
   c. Woodbury.
   d. Woods.

help: Search by phrase *wimbledon* then *queen and*


574. What was NOT true about 1907 Rose Queen Joan Woodbury?
   a. Her robe was white.
   b. Her flowers were California poppies.
   c. She picked her own court.
   d. She was single.

**1900**

help: *roses, 1907 - Queen*


575. Although not necessarily a Pasadena resident, which Babe participated in the 1944 Pasadena City Men's Golf Tournament at Brookside Golf Course?
   a. Didrikson.
   b. Horrell.
   c. Ruth.
   d. Zaharias.

**1940**

help: *men's golf* then *babe*

18th Fairway Brookside Golf Courses. 1945.

ppl_8351

576. For the 1908 Rose Parade, how were members of the Rose Court, other than the Queen, selected?
   a. Each High School got to pick one.
   b. The Queen got to pick.
   c. The same person who picked the Queen got to pick the Court.
   d. They had a popularity contest and they came in 2 through 6.

help: *1908 - Queen* then *court*


577. The Marines of Mare Island invaded Pasadena twice by train, once in 1917 and then again in 1918. Why?
   a. Pasadena has a football game on New Year's Day.
   b. Pasadena girls are pretty.
   c. They were determined to get it right.
   d. The Army said they couldn't.

**1910**

help: Search by phrase *mare island*


578. What is the last name of the Rose Queen who walked through the "Stage Door Canteen" and into a career as a film star?
   a. Dougall.
   b. Moore.
   c. Nichols.
   d. Walker.

help: *queen and* then *stage door*


579. Name a place in Pasadena where an airplane has NOT landed
   a. Arroyo Parkway.
   b. Brookside Golf Course.
   c. Colorado Boulevard.
   d. Tournament Park.

help: *Airplane* then *land*

580. When he was stopped, James E. Fronimos would have been charged with drunk driving on Arroyo Parkway in 1947, except one thing flummoxed the police. What was it?
   a. His dad was the police chief.
   b. He was a very convincing actor.
   c. He was in an airplane.
   d. He was joining the Army the next day.

**1940**

help: *fronimos*


581. Which former head of the Pasadena Chamber of Commerce was exiled to Honolulu in 1952?
   a. C. Hal Reynolds.
   b. Carl E. Wopshall.
   c. Stanley C. Van Dyke.
   d. Walter Stuart Young.

**1950**

help: *chamber of comm* then *exiled*


582. In 1915, School Superintendent Jeremiah M. Rhodes said running out of what would cause the schools to close?
   a. Money.
   b. Teachers.
   c. Textbooks.
   d. Vaccinations.

**1910**

help: *rhodes* then *close*

583. In early 1942 (after Pearl Harbor) what changes were made to the Pasadena Police Pistol Range in Eaton Canyon that took three weeks to implement?
    a. A concrete barrier was built to protect observers.
    b. It was rebuilt to include rifles.
    c. The targets were made to look Japanese.
    d. Use was restricted to daylight hours because of the blackout.

**1940**

help: *pistol range* then *three weeks*


584. The city used to own an outdoor firing range in Eaton Canyon (the Pasadena Police Pistol Range). In 2004, the city responded to four years of complaints by residents about safety and noise pollution problems by doing what?
    a. Moving it indoors.
    b. Restricting the hours of operation.
    c. Shutting it down.
    d. Using the complainers as targets.

**2000**

help: *pistol range* then *complaints*


585. Which Pasadena property was "reported" to have been bought by John D. Rockefeller in 1906?
    a. Brookside Park.
    b. Busch Gardens.
    c. Carmelita Park.
    d. La Pintoresca Hotel.

**1900**

help: *feller* then *bought*

586. Which golf course was the site of a "brutal" murder in 1906?
   a. Annandale.
   b. Brookside.
   c. Huntington Hotel.
   d. Raymond Hotel.

**1900**

help: *murder* then *golf*

587. After his visit in 1903, John D. Rockefeller donated one thousand dollars to
   a. Carmelita Park.
   b. First Baptist Church.
   c. Pasadena Public Library.
   d. Shakespeare Club.

**1900**

help: *feller* then *one thousand*

588. In 2013, Tracey Cooper-Harris won a case on same-sex marriage as it related to
   a. Child custody.
   b. Income tax.
   c. Medical benefits.
   d. Veteran benefits.

**2010**

help: *Cooper-Harris*

589. Should the police be paid when ill (sick time) was a question for the mayor in
   a. 1904.
   b. 1914.
   c. 1924.
   d. 1934.

help: *police department* then *paid when ill*

590. Which city department was proclaimed "first place in class" in 1942
   a. Fire.
   b. Library.
   c. Police.
   d. Power.

**1940**

help: *Municipal officials* then *first place in class*


591. During the influenza epidemic, 1918-1919, the library was closed for about
   a. Four hours.
   b. Four days.
   c. Four weeks.
   d. Four months.

**1910**

help: *pasadena public library* then *1918-1919*


592. The upside for library management of being closed down by the influenza epidemic, 1918-1919, was that the library was able to
   a. Add a reading room.
   b. Clean out the basement.
   c. Finally get all the books back on the shelf.
   d. Have a full month of staff development days.

**1910**

help: *library* then *1918-1919*

*This photo looks like it was taken outside the library in now what is known as Memorial Park. Then it was called Library Park. During the influenza epidemic, maskes were required for people appearing in public.*

*ppl_3905*

593. Before being closed by the influenza epidemic, 1918-1919, there were certain restrictions put in place at the library. Because of the outbreak, what was no longer allowed after October 17, 1918, at the Pasadena Public Library?
    a. Checking out books at the library.
    b. Complaining to the librarians.
    c. Reading at the library.
    d. Talking at the library.

**1910**

help; Limit by dates from 10/17/1918 to 10/ 31/1918 then *pasadena public library*


594. In 1918, how many books did the Pasadena Public Library children's dept. have?
    a. 900.
    b. 5,000.
    c. 9,000.
    d. 15,000.

**1910**

help: *public lib* then *dept.*

595. What marred the visit James Logan (an African American) made to the Raymond Hotel's golf course in 1906?
    a. His golf score.
    b. His green fees.
    c. His murder.
    d. His treatment by his caddy.

**1900**

help: *Logan, james* then *golf*

596. The Kathleen of Kathleen's on Lake is
   a. Kathleen, a legal corporation.
   b. Kathleen Brown, a dog.
   c. Kathleen Leggs, a spider.
   d. Kathleen Meymerian, a person.

help: Search by phrase *kathleen's on lake*


597. During the Zoot Suit Riots during World War Two soldiers chased and beat up young Hispanic men because of the clothes they wore (zoot suits). In June of 1943, two "Zooters" were chased by 150 soldiers into the Pasadena police station. What happened to the soldiers?
   a. They forfeited a night of dancing.
   b. They had to listen to a lecture about Hispanic culture.
   c. They turned around and went looking for other Hispanics to chase.
   d. They were shipped out to the Pacific.

**1940**

phrase: Search by phrase *zooters*


598. Because of a court order, in 1970, Pasadena conducted a nationwide search for Hispanic and African American what?
   a. Jurors.
   b. Librarians.
   c. Police officers.
   d. Teachers.

**1970**

help: Search by phrase *wide search*


599. What sport had its inaugural debut in the Rose Bowl in 1932?
   a. Cricket.
   b. Dog racing.
   c. Polo.
   d. Soccer.

**1930**

help: *Rose bowl, 1932* then *inaugural*

600. What school threatened to move to the Rose Bowl because they it wanted greater control over its "home" stadium in 1932?
   a. Pasadena City College.
   b. Occidental College.
   c. UCLA.
   d. USC.

**1930**

help: *rose bowl, 1932* then *threat*


601. Miss La Vieve M. Hines used what to win the first World Congress for Women in at the Maryland Hotel in 1932?
   a. Pieces shaped like a castle.
   b. Pieces shaped like a coin.
   c. Pieces shaped like a shoe.
   d. Pieces with letters on them.

**1930**

help: *hines, La Vieve*


602. In 1950, who was Fox Field named after?
   a. Charles J. Fox, sportsman.
   b. Daniel F. Fox, pastor.
   c. John E. Fox, policeman.
   d. Orrin Russell Fox, Jr., war hero.

**1950**

help: Seatch by phrase *fox field*


603. Who was the Fox Cup named after?
   a. Charles J. Fox, sportsman.
   b. Daniel F. Fox, pastor.
   c. John E. Fox, policeman.
   d. Orrin Russell Fox, Jr., war hero.

help: *fox cup*

604. (Fill in the blank to this 1970 *Pasadena Star-News* article.) "Buses to integrate 14,500 Pasadena pupils: _____ 'Runs' needed to do job. "
   a. 300.
   b. 600.
   c. 1200.
   d. 1800.

**1970**
help: Search by phrase *14,500*

*The tavern at Brook side Park Plunge, which was for many years a segregated facility. This picture maybe from around the time it was reopened as an integrated facility, June 7, 1947.*
*ppl_3591*

Match the following answers to the questions 605-617. Each answer is a fact about a Pasadena city manager (The years provided are the years they were city manager). For help with each question, combine the subject search term *city manager* with an element from the hint.

    a. After Pasadena, Covina looked pretty good.
    b. After Pasadena, Long Beach (its newspaper even) looked pretty good.
    c. After Pasadena, Saudi Arabia looked pretty good.
    d. After Pasadena, the American Red Cross looked pretty good.
    e. After Pasadena, the Pasadena Art Museum looked pretty good.
    f. After Pasadena, the University of La Verne looked pretty good.
    g. Before he was city manager, he had the idea to run city cars on natural gas.
    h. "Four Horsemen" against him; "Three Musketeers" for him. He soon quit.
    i. Married woman should not be employed by the city.
    j. Thought Berkeley and Pasadena were alike.
    k. While in Pasadena, Iraq also looked pretty good.
    l. While in Riverside, Pasadena looked pretty good.
    m. Worked to employ disabled veterans.

*Fountain at City Hall*
*ppl_94*

605. C. Wellington Koiner, 1921-1925; 1933 to 1946
Answer: _____

606. Robert Vance Orbison, 1925-1931
Answer: _____

607. John W. Charleville, 1931-1933
Answer: _____

608. Harold M. Hines, 1946-1947
Answer: _____

609. Robert M. McCurdy, 1947-1948 (interim)
Answer: _____

610. Don C. McMillan, 1948-1963
Answer: _____

611. Elder Gunter, 1963-1966
Answer: _____

612. John D. Phillips, 1966-1973
Answer: _____

613. Don McIntyre 1973-1990
Answer: _____

614. Phillip Hawkey, 1990-1998
Answer: _____

615. Cynthia Kurtz, 1998-2008
Answer: _____

616. Bernard Melekian, 2008 (interim)
Answer: _____

617. Michael Beck, 2008-
Answer: _____

618. During World War I, German spies were said to be stealing from Pasadena
  a. Banks.
  b. Libraries.
  c. Military recruiting facilities.
  d. Schools.

help: Search by phrase *german spies*


619. When it opened in 1990, the new state-of-the-art Pasadena jail had no
  a. Bars.
  b. Beds.
  c. Doors.
  d. Internet.

help: Limit by date to 1990 then search by phrase *jail*


620. Why were members of the Pasadena City Council thrown in jail in October, 1984?
  a. The police had worked two years without a contract and were frustrated.
  b. Someone noticed they had neglected to pay their parking tickets for a long time.
  c. To demonstrate that, despite all the bad publicity about the building, it really wasn't that bad.
  d. To drum up publicity for Proposition DD to raise money for a new jail.

help: *city council* then *in jail*

621. In 1899 work was started on an elevated track meant primarily for
   a. Automobiles
   b. Bicycles.
   c. Pedestrians
   b. Railroads.

**1890**

help: Search by phrase *elevated track*


622. During World War I, City Librarian Nellie Russ said that "Teutonic Philosophy" had no place at the Pasadena Public Library. So she
   a. Cancelled the library's annual participation in Oktoberfest.
   b. Changed "Hamburgers" to "Pasadenaburgers" in the card catalogue.
   c. "Interned" German books.
   d. Took away the library cards of German Americans.

**1910**

help: Search by phrase *teutonic*


623. In January 1941 the first Pasadena radio quiz show was broadcast over station KPPC. Which Pasadena group backed it?
   a. Pasadena Chamber of Commerce.
   b. Pasadena Lions Club.
   c. Pasadena Public Library.
   d. Women's Civic League.

**1940**

help: Search by phrase *radio quiz*


624. In 1924, radio station KPPC was started by the
   a. Pasadena Playhouse.
   b. Pasadena Public Library.
   c. Pasadena Presbyterian Church.
   d. Pasadena Police Department.

**1920**

help: *kppc* then scroll to bottom of page.

625. In 1973, radio station KPPC became radio station
   a. KIIS.
   b. KMET.
   c. KODJ.
   d. KROQ.

**1970**

help: Limit by date to 1973 then *KPPC*


626. In 1942, radio station KPCC broadcast an episode called "Home Garden." It was part of a larger radio program produced by the Pasadena Defense Council to support the home front during World War Two: What was the name of that program?
   a. Pasadena at War.
   b. Tips to Victory.
   c. United for Victory.
   d. Victory at Home.

**1940**

help: *kpcc* then *home garden*


627. How many giant bells did Samuel L. Allen have at his command when he played them at Pasadena Presbyterian Church over radio station KPPC in 1939?
   a. 1.
   b. 5.
   c. 11.
   d. 15.

**1930**

help: *allen, samuel*

*Presbyterian Church (2nd building Colorado and Worcester (now Garfield) 1890.*

*ppl_3627*

628. Which President, who after visiting Pasadena, called it "Garden of the Lord"?
   a. Benjamin Harrison.
   b. Rutherford Birchard Hayes.
   c. Theodore Roosevelt.
   d. William Howard Taft.

help: *presidents - journeys* then *of the Lord*


629. In 1947, Wesley Glass, an African American who fought in World War Two, faced racial discrimination in Pasadena when he tried to
   a. Find a place to live.
   b. Get a job.
   c. Get married.
   d. Go to school.

**1940**

help: *glass, wes*


630. After World War Two there were many shortages for the returning vets. In 1946 the City Council spent $9000 to ease problems in the area of
   a. Education.
   b. Employment.
   c. Housing.
   d. Recreation.

**1940**

help: *city council* then *9000*


631. What location was described by the *Pasadena Post* in 1939 as the "city's 'musical landmark'"?
   a. The bells at Pasadena Presbyterian Church.
   b. The bells at Saint Andrew's Church.
   c. The organ at Neighborhood Church.
   d. The organ at the Raymond Theater.

**1930**

help: Search by phrase *musical landmark*

632. As President William Howard Taft bid farewell Pasadena in 1909, the last thing he probably heard was
    a. May Sutton congratulating Hazel Hotchkiss on their exhibition tennis match for the president.
    b. The elderly gentlemen of the Grand Army of the Republic who had formed his honor guard taking a nap.
    c. The sounds of banks opening that had been closed during his visit.
    d. The sounds of the bells of Pasadena Presbyterian Church playing "Hail to the Chief."

**1900**

help: *taft, william* then *farewell*


633. My name was William Auman.
    My uniform the color of fawn.
    I went off to Cuba,
    Not to play the tuba,
    But to charge up a hill at San _____ .
    Answer: _____

**1890**

help: *auman,* then *san*


634. In response to a severe housing shortage after World War Two, the City Council in 1945 passed an emergency housing law to allow people to live in what?
    a. Home garages.
    b. Storage units.
    c. Tents.
    d. Trailers.

**1940**

help: Search by phrase *emergency housing law*

635. (Fill in the blank.) Jane Hunt gave her _____ to the library in 1908.
    a. Books.
    b. Dogs.
    c. Money.
    d. Paintings.

**1900**

help: *hunt, jane*


636. (Fill in the blank.) In July 1998, City Councilman William Paparian announced his _____ trip to Cuba.
a. 1st
b. 2nd.
c. 5th.
d. 7th.

**1990**

help: limit date to July 1998 then *paparian* then *Cuba*


637. (Fill in the blank.) Between its incorporation in March of 1942 and February of 1943, the Pasadena Hospitality House (which was a place for soldiers to go sponsored by the women of Pasadena) hosted _____ soldiers
    a. 700.
    b. 7,000.
    c. 70,000.
    d. 700,000.

**1940**

help: Limit by end date to 03/01/1943 then *hospitality house*


638. Upon his return from World War Two, disabled vet Richard C. Atkins began to work using a
    a. Little black book.
    b. Microphone.
    c. Motar and pestle.
    d. Wrench.

**1940**

help: *Atkins, Ri*

639. (Fill in the blank.) In 2013 dollars, During World War Two, Pasadenans bought at least _____ worth of government bonds (use 1945 as a year of comparison):
    a. $7,330,000.
    b. $73,300,000.
    c. $733,000,000.
    d. $7,330,000,000.

**1940**

help: *1939-1945* then *bonds*; add; then Google *current value of a dollar*, then convert at a web site like measuringworth.com/uscompare


640. Of that amount from question 639, at least how much came from city departments (again converting 1945 dollars to 2013 dollars):
    a. $72,800.
    b. $728,000.
    c. $7,280,000.
    d. $72,280,000.

**1940**

help: *1939-1945 then bonds*; add; then Google *current value of a dollar*, then convert at a web site like measuringworth.com/uscompare


641. Florence Lowe, famous Pasadena aviatrix (pilot), thought she would make a very good what in 1932?
    a. County supervisor.
    b. Policewoman.
    c. City council member.
    d. President of the Chamber of Commerce.

**1930**

help: *lowe, flo* then *aviatrix*

642. Peter Boncheff was visited by a member of a gang at his business in 1932, and it was "suggested" that he pay $5 a month in extortion, and that other businesses in Mr. Boncheff's line of work would making a similar contribution. What was Mr. Boncheff's business called?
   a. New Europe Cafe.
   b. New Europe Salon.
   c. New Europe Market.
   d. New Europe Auto Repair.

**1930**

help: *boncheff,*


643. The "Pasadena Handicap" that took place in the Braley Building in 1932 was actually
   a. A fundraising event by the Chamber of Commerce
   b. A party for debutantes by La Floristas.
   c. A sting operation by the police department.
   d. An educational event for youth by the library.

**1930**

help: *Braley build* then *handicap*


644. In 1932, famous Caltech physicist Robert Millikan offered to analyze the radium in local water. He wanted to know
   a. If it were bottled would it be safe to drink.
   b. If there were any potential commercial applications.
   c. If it could help find one's pet in the dark.
   d. If people living near Caltech had anything to worry about in terms of water quality.

**1930**

help: *millikan* then *radium*

645. I was an American President.
   I was supposed to have stayed at the Maryland Hotel in 1923, but I didn't show up.
   Mayor Hiram Wadsworth said very nice things about me when I didn't appear.
   What is my last name?
   Answer:_____

**1920**

help: Limit by date to 1923, then *presidents - journeys* then *Wadsworth, hir*


646. In 2002, an avocado-eating bear left the neighborhood he had been staying in because
   a. The deputies arrived.
   b. The salsa was too mild.
   c. They ran out of avocados.
   d. They refused to give him chips.

**2000**

help: *bears* then *avocado*


647. In 1915 what Pasadena artist was called by the Pasadena Star 'America's leading portrait painter'?
   a. Benjamin Brown
   b. C. P. Townsley
   c. Elmer Wachtel
   d. Jean Mannheim

**1910**

help: *artist* then *leading portrait*

648. One of the stated plans of the newly formed Cauldron Club in 1911 was to create a club of people who could best be described as
   a. Elephants.
   b. Hams.
   c. Monkeys.
   d. Song birds.

help: Limit by date to 1911 then *cauldron*


649. Reading the *Pasadena Star-News* in 1916, what animal would you think of when you read about the Americus Club?
   a. Eagle.
   b. Elephant.
   c. Monkey.
   d. Song bird.

help: Limit by date to 1916 then *americus*


650. Which Van Nuys firm was probably glad when James E. Spangler left a federal court in 1970?
   a. Anheuser-Busch.
   b. Embree Bus Company.
   c. McGraw-Hill Textbook Company.
   d. Sparkletts Water Company.

help: *Spangler* then *Van Nuys*


651. Wilson J. Lee, who had an abscess pressing on his brain, was permitted to return early from the Spanish-American War with permission from
   a. George Dewey.
   b. Theodore Roosevelt.
   c. William McKinley.
   d. William R. Shafter.

help: *Lee, Wilson*

652. In 1935 at Central Park, the United States defeated the Canadians in
   a. Bicycling.
   b. Chess.
   c. Croquet.
   d. Lawn bowling.

**1930**

help: *central park* then *canadians*


653. In 1925, Mrs. J. C. Dunn visited her sister Mrs. C. B. Harrison in Pasadena and proclaimed publicly her desire for young men. Why?
   a. As the owner of a baseball team, she thought younger players would be better for her team.
   b. As the owner of a restaurant, she thought they would attract customers.
   c. As the owner of a school, she believed in co-education.
   d. As a widow, well, you know.

**1920**

help: *Dunn, Mrs. J. C.*


654. What per cent of Pasadena's population was eligible for the draft for World War One?
   a. A little less than 3 per cent.
   b. A little less than 5 per cent.
   c. A little less than 10 per cent.
   d. A little less than 15 per cent.

**1910**

help: *1914-1918* then *per cent*


655. Raul T. Reynolds was
   a. An African American who fought in the Battle of Argonne (1918).
   b. An African American who fought in the Battle of Khe Sanh (1968).
   c. An African American who fought in the battle of Pork Chop Hill (1953).
   d. An African American who fought in the Battle of San Juan Hill (1898).

help: *Reynolds, Raul*

656. Which Pasadena junior high school had a class in flying and built a plane?
    a. George Washington.
    b. Charles W. Eliot.
    c. William McKinley.
    d. Woodrow Wilson.

help: *junior high* then *plane*


657. In 1911, schools had vocational education targeting boys who expressed a desire to use what?
    a. Airplanes.
    b. Hoes.
    c. Lathes.
    d. Stoves.

help: *vocational* then *boys*


658. In 1920, for her class in vocational education for Hispanic Americans at the Mexican Settlement House, Miss Autin needed what kind of material?
    a. Fabric.
    b. Food.
    c. Looms.
    d. Seeds.

help: *autin, miss*


659. The Cinco de Mayo celebration of which year had nearly 1000 participants?
a. 1911.
b. 1931.
c. 1951.
d. 1971.

help: *cinco de* then *1000*

660. One can only hope that the students of Pasadena Part-Time School were paying full-time attention when they built what in class?
a. Airplanes.
b. Automobiles.
c. Power plants.
d. Speed boats.

help: *pasadena part-time*


661. (Fill in the blank.) Justin _____ and Jay-Z were scheduled to play in the Rose Bowl in 2013.
   a. Bieber.
   b. Long.
   c. Moore.
   d. Timberlake.

**2010**

help: *jay-z*


662. I was a Prima Donna,
   but not in a conceited way.
   I sang at Pasadena High School in 1915,
   but I wasn't a student there.
   I was famous for the Chocolate Soldier
   but not in a candy way.
   What was my last name?
   Answer:_____

**1910**

help: *pasadena high school* then *prima donna*

663. In 2009 it was reported that what concert was going to be the biggest in Rose Bowl history (at least up until 2009)?
   a. Guns 'n Roses.
   b. Journey.
   c. Rolling Stones.
   d. U2.

**2000**

help: *rose bowl, 2009* then *biggest in*


664. Which of these is NOT true about President Herbert Hoover's visit to Pasadena in November 1932?
   a. He met the 1933 Rose Queen Dorothy Edwards.
   b. He met the Mayor E. O. Nay.
   c. He spoke in front of City Hall.
   d. He was hoping to be re-elected President.

**1930**

help: limit by dates to November 1932, then *hoover, herbert*


665. (Fill in the blank.) In 1921, Fran Tolley Brand wanted to be the first woman to _____ across America.
   a. Drive.
   b. Fly.
   c. Hitch-hike.
   d. Walk.

**1920**

help: *brand, fran*

*Scan from the article "Air Craft for Travel and Post" by Wayne Alles, Sales Manager Mercury Aviation Company, appearing in California Southland, February / March 1920 p. 19*

ppl_10737

CROWDS ATTENDING THE OPENING OF PASADENA'S FLYING FIELD, THE FIRST MUNICIPAL FLYING FIELD IN CALIFORNIA

666. (Fill in the blank.) In 1932, Pasadena pilot Melba Gorby wanted to make her plane go _____ than any plane like it had gone before.
   a. Faster.
   b. Higher.
   c. Longer.
   d. Farther on a gallon of fuel.

**1930**

help: *Gorby, melba*


667. Which candidate for president took a campaign swing through Pasadena in 1976?
   a. Gerald Ford.
   b. Jerry Brown.
   c. Jimmy Carter.
   d. Ronald Reagan.

**1970**

help: *elections, 1976*


668. The federal court ordered that Pasadena schools be integrated in 1970. The ACLU Pasadena/Foothill Chapter paid off the last part of its portion of the court cost in
   a. 1970.
   b. 1973.
   c. 1977.
   d. 1979.

**1970**

help: *school integration* then *court cost*

669. (Fill in the blanks.) Jared Sidney _____ of Pasadena founded the city of _____ in 1912
   a. Bell/Bell.
   b. Chandler/Chandler.
   c. Reseda/Reseda.
   d. Torrance/Torrance.

**1910**

help: search by phrase *jared sidney* then *city of*


670. What famed film director used "a cast of thousands" and the night and the Pasadena Civic Auditorium as a film location in 1977?
   a. Francis Ford Coppola.
   b. John Cassavetes.
   c. Martin Scorcese.
   d. Sam Peckinpah.

**1970**

help: *location* then *cast of thousands*


671. In 1977, Ben Holt Engineering was going to study what kind of energy source for the Pasadena Water and Power Department?
   a. Geothermal.
   b. Nuclear.
   c. Solar.
   d. Wind.

**1970**

help: *Ben holt*


672. Ex-Pasadena city employee Charles Bereal was arrested for attacking which city manager in 1977?
   a. Don McIntyre.
   b. Don C. McMillan.
   c. John D. Phillips.
   d. John William Charleville.

**1970**

help: *bereal, charles* then *city manager*

673. (Fill in the blank.) Where the Paseo Colorado currently is located, there once was the Plaza Pasadena Mall. One idea that was proposed was to have a "Hall of _____" built on the roof of the mall.
    a. Science.
    b. Shame.
    c. Shoes.
    d. Slurpies.

**1970**

help: *plaza pasadena* then *hall of*


674. (Fill in the blank.) 1998 QE2 is a monster _____ that could have destroyed Earth, but didn't, in 2013.
    a. Asteroid rock.
    b. Computer virus.
    c. Manga character.
    d. Monetary union.

**2010**

help: *QE2*


675. In 1929, the Pasadena Playhouse put out a call for Mexican actors for its forthcoming production of
    a. "Eden."
    b. "Macbeth."
    c. "The Mikado."
    d. "Uncle Tom's Cabin."

**1920**

help: *pasadena playhouse* then *mexican*

676. In 1931, Eva Lopez returned to Pasadena with high honors for her work in
   a. Sales.
   b. School.
   c. Sewing.
   d. Social work.

**1930**

help: *lopez, eva*


677. In 1938, the Mexican Settlement House was denied a permit to operate on California Street. The stated reason was that residents already there said that the House would
   a. Be a nuisance.
   b. Encourage loitering.
   c. Increase traffic.
   d. Lower property values.

**1930**

help: *settlement house* then *deny*


678. A 1934 show by the Pasadena Settlement Association of Mexican arts and crafts was successful in showing
   a. Culture.
   b. Diversity.
   c. Music.
   d. Workmanship.

**1930**

help: *settlement assoc* then *in showing*

679. (Fill in the blank.) A 1977 *Pasadena Star-News* headline said the new Commission of the Status of Women rejected a "radical image." According to the headline the Commission was looking for a _____ Coordinator.
    a. Good-looking.
    b. Open-minded.
    c. Pragmatic.
    d. Well-balanced.

**1970**

help: *status of women* then *radical image*


680. What peril bit three persons in Eaton Canyon in 1979?
    a. Bats.
    b. Coyotes.
    c. Dogs.
    d. Rats.

**1970**

help: *eaton canyon* then *peril*


681. In 1979, people interested in what issue vowed a ballot fight against City Council member Don Yokaitis?
    a. Northwest development.
    b. Overnight parking.
    c. Rent control.
    d. Use of the Rose Bowl.

**1970**

help: *yokait* then *ballot fight*

682. According to a 1979 *Pasadena Star-News* headline, who was fearing expulsion from Fuller Theology Seminary?
   a. African Americans.
   b. Democrats.
   c. Gays.
   d. Muslims.

help: *Fuller theo* then *expulsion*


683. Women of Pasadean City College fell five points short of winning the state title in what sport in 1979?
   a. Basketball.
   b. Softball.
   c. Swimming.
   d. Track.

help: *City college* then *five points*


684. Chris Gobrecht coached the same sport at USC and PCC. The sport involved
   a. Racing about a track.
   b. Racing around a diamond.
   c. Racing on hardwood.
   d. Racing through water.

help: *Gobrecht* then *usc*


685. Which U.S. president was invited, but sent only his regrets to attend a Rose Parade? (Meaning he didn't show up.)
   a. Dwight D. Eisenhower.
   b. Herbert Hoover.
   c. Richard Nixon.
   d. Theodore Roosevelt.

help: *of roses* then *regrets*

686. Which U.S. president was invited twice to be Grand Marshal of the Rose Parade, but did it only once?
    a. Dwight D. Eisenhower.
    b. Herbert Hoover.
    c. Richard Nixon.
    d. Theodore Roosevelt.

help: *of roses* then *presidents* then scan list


687. Which U.S. president was invited twice to be Grand Marshal of the Rose Parade, and did it both times?
    a. Dwight D. Eisenhower.
    b. Herbert Hoover.
    c. Richard Nixon.
    d. Theodore Roosevelt.

help: *of roses* then *presidents* then scan list


688. Which U.S. president was invited only once to be Grand Marshal, and did it the only time he was asked?
    a. Dwight D. Eisenhower.
    b. Herbert Hoover.
    c. Richard Nixon.
    d. Theodore Roosevelt.

help: *of roses* then *presidents* then scan list

689. When in office I visited Pasadena where
    I gave a speech at Caltech backing big science
    I was jeered at a World Cup Soccer match (but U.S. beat China)
    And I was accused of being shy
    What is my last name?
a. Carter.
b. Clinton.
c. Ford.
d. Hoover.

help: *presidents* then *shy*


690. I've been called Grace
    I've been called Pasadena Art Museum
    Now I am called Norton
    Do you know where I now Be-un?
        Answer: _____ (three words)

help: *Pasadena art museum* then *norton*

*This is when he was Grand Marshall in 1953.*

*ppl_h2403*

# Answers to quiz questions

1:b 2:c 3:d 4:a 5:d 6:b 7:a 8:b 9:b 10:b 11:a 12:c 13: b 14:b 15:c 16:a 17:c 18:c 19:Michelson

20:d 21:b 22:c 23:d 24:b 25:d 26:c 27:c 28:a 29:c 30:a 31:b 32:d 33.a 34:Sirhan

35:a 36:c 37: Moussa, Angell,Wallens, Jack

38:c 39:a 40:b 41:d 42:b 43:New York Drive

44:d 45:b 46:c 47:a 48:c 49:c 50:a 51:c 52:b 53:Americanization

54:b 55:c 56:d 57:d 58:a 59:c 60:b 61:d 62:d 63:d 64:b 65:d 66:c 67:b 68:a 69:d 70:d 71:b 72:d 73:a 74:c 75:d 76:c 77:c 78:d 79:Sirhan

80:c 81:a 82:d 83:c 84:c 85.c 86.b 87:c 88:c 89.c 90:a 91:c 92:a 93:a 94:b 95.c 96:c 97:a 98:central library

99:b 100:d 101:c 102:c 103:d 104:b 105:a 106:d 107:b 108:c 109:c 110:b 111:c 112:a 113:c 114:c 115:a 116:d 117:d 118:a 119:c 120:d 121:a 122:c 123:c 124:Pauley

125:c 126:c 127:b 128:c 129:c 130:c 131:d 132:b 133:c 134:c 135:c 136:d 137:d 138:a 139:d 140:b 141:c 142:b 143:d 144:c 145:b 146:a 147:b 148:traffic protection

149:d 150:c 151:a 152:a 153:b 154:d 155:d 156:d 157:a 158:d 159:b 160:c 161:a 162:b 163:a 164:a 165:a 166:d 167:b 168:b 169:a 170:d 171:c 172:Coleman

173:c 174:c 175:a 176:c 177:b 178:b 179:d 180:d 181:d 182:c 183:c 184:a 185:a 186:b 187:d 188:d 189:c 190:a 191:b 192:a 193:b 194:b 195:a 196:d 197:b 198:b 199:b 200:d 201:c 202:Reagan

203:c 204:b 205:c 206:d 207:b 208:a 209:b 210:c 211:c 212:b 213:b 214:a  215:d 216:c 217:c 218:a 219:a 220:b 221:d 222:d 223:b 224:b 225:d 226:c 227:d 228:c 229:c 230:e 231:a 232:Pasadena (Ship)

233:b 234:d 235:c 236:c 237:c 238:d 239:b 240:a 241:b 242:c 243:a 244:b 245:b 246:a 247:b 248:b 249:d 250:c 251:d 252:a 253:a 254:a 255:c 256:b 257:d 258:Zornes

259:a 260:b 261:c 262:d 263:c 264:b 265:a 266:a 267:c 268:a 269:c 270:b 271:a 272:d 273:a 274:a 275:ball

276:c 277:d 278:a 279:d 280:c 281:d 282:b 283:a 284:b 285:d 286:c 287:c 288:d 289:c 290:a 291:c 292:b 293:a 294:c 295:b 296:d 297:a 298:b 299:b 300:d 301:e 302:c 303:b 304:d 305:d 306:b 307:d 308:a 309:c 310:c 311:a 312:b 313:a 314:d 315:a 316:a 317:c 318:Foot-and-Mouth Disease

319:a 320:a 321:a 322:d 323:d 324:e 325:a 326:c 327:d 328:a 329:c 330:c 331:c 332:a 333:c 334:c 335:b 336:a 337:a 338:b 339:d 340:c 341:b 342:d

343:c 344:c 345:a 346:a 347:c 348:b 349:a 350:c 351:a 352:c 353:a 354:d 355:d 356:b 357:d 358:b 359:a 360:d 361:c 362:b 363:b 364:a 365:Farnsworth

366:c 367:c 368:c 369:a 370:c 371:a 372:a 373:a 374:d 375:a 376:b 377:c 378:c 379:c 380:c 381:b 382:b 383:a 384:c 385:b 386:d 387:c 388:b 389:b 390:c 391:a 392:b

393:d 394:d 395:d 396:d 397:b 398:a 399:c 400:a 401:c 402:d 403:c 404:c 405:c 406:c 407:a 408:d 409:c 410:d 411:b 412:d 413:d 414:a 415:a 416:a 417:a 418:c 419:d 420:c 421:d 422:c 423:b 424:d 425:farrell
426:c 427:c 428:c 429:b 430:d 431:c 432:b 433:a 434:b 435:d 436:c 437:b 438:b 439:a 440:Berardino

441:b 442:c 443:b 444:c 445:d 446:d 447:b 448:a 449:d 450:b 451:c 452:b 453:c 454:b 455:c 456:a 457:a 458:a 459:d 460:e 461:a 462:d 463:c 464:b 465:c 466:d 467:b

468:c 469:c 470:d 471:c 472:a 473:d 474:b 475:d 476:a 477:b 478:c 479:a 480:a 481:d 482:c 483:c 484:richter

485:c 486:a 487:c 488:b 489:c 490:b 491:d 492:c 493:b 494:a 495:b 496:b 497:d 498:d 499:c 500:d 501:a 502:b 503:b 504:a 505:b 506:a 507:c 508:b 509:d 510:Miller
511:b 512:c 513:d 514:n 515:c 516:c 517:a 518:a 519:a 520:c 521:b 522:d 523:d 524:b 525:a 526:slavin

527:b 528:c 529:b 530:c 531:c 532:a 533:b 534:b 535:b 536:b 537:c 538:d 539:c 540:c 541:d 542:c 543:d 544:c 545:c 546:d 547:d 548:b 549:c 550:d 551:c 552:b 553:c 554:a 555:cobi

556:b 557:c 558:d 559:b 560:c 561:b 562:Lee

563:d 564:c 565:c 566:d 567:c 568:c 569:c 570:d 571:a 572:b 573:a 574:d 575:d 576:b 577:a 578:d 579:c 580:c 581:c 582:a 583:b 584:a 585:c 586:d 587:b 588:d 589:a 590:b 591:c 592:a 593:c 594:c 595:c 596:d

597:a 598:d 599:a 600:d 601:a 602:d 603:a 604:b 605:g 606:h 607:i 608:b 609:m 610:e 611:c 612:j 613:d 614:f 615:a 616:k 617:l 618:b 619:a 620:d 621:b 622:c 623:b 624:c 625:d 626:c 627:c 628:c 629:a 630:c 631:a 632:d 633:juan

634:a 635:d 636:d 637:c 638:a 639:a 640:c 641:a 642:a 643:c 644:a 645:harding

646:a 647:d 648:b 649:b 650:b 651:c 652:d 653:a 654:c 655:a 656:a 657:d 658:c 659:b 660:a 661:d 662:kopetzky

663:d 664:d 665:b 666:b 667:a 668:c 669:d 670:b 671:a 672:a 673:a 674:a 675:a 676:b 677:d 678:d 679:b 680:b 681:c 682:c 683:a 684:c 685:d 686:a 687:c 688:b 689:b 690:norton simon museum

# Index

(Please note. An item is not placed in the index if putting it in the index would reveal the answer. Also items placed after the main subject heading can encompass items mentioned in the subheadings.)

Allen, Samuel L.: 627
Alexander, Frank: 82
Ames, Thomas W.: 317
Animals: 162, 163, 277, 387, 421, 466, 483, 680,
    Bears: 646
    Birds: 249,
    Cows: 133, 134, 318
    Dogs: 206, 207, 350, 351, 412
    Horses: 12, 174, 365, 385
Art & Entertainment: 54, 144, 240, 361, 385, 386, 394, 395, 419, 465, 530, 557, 648
    Art: 19, 20, 116, 138, 139, 191, 258, 405, 647, 690
    Award ceremonies: 117
    Books: 263, 457, 484, 558, 569, 594, 622
    California Philharmonic Orchestra: 180
    Circuses: 146,
    Conventions: 47; 48, 120, 227
    Debates: 393
    Events (non rose Parade): 129, 158, 160, 195, 275, 392, 547, 570
    Memorials: 43, 107, 333, 436, 437, 459
    Music: 44, 45, 65, 66, 145, 155, 180, 182, 203, 214, 215, 234, 256, 297, 298, 348, 349, 506, 627, 631, 661, 662, 663
    Plays: 210, 364, 440, 525, 537, 539, 548, 571, 572, 675
    Public Art: 77, 114
    Sculpture: 301
Atkins, Richard C.: 638
Auman, William: 633

Baker, Mary Dell: 136
Balazs, Alejandro: 189
Ballhorn, Mary: 351
Barker, Alice: 142
Barnhart, George E. Eddie: 372, 381

Barnes, Florence: 641
Barrett, Richard J.: 464
Beal, William A.: 475
Beck, Michael: 617
Becker, Fred H., Jr.: 327
Bell, Kenneth: 373
Bennett, Barbara, 264
Bergman, Rey: 93
Blake, Geoffrey: 95
Blecksmith, James: 322
Boncheff, Peter: 642
Bontempo, David Patrick: 332
Bourne, A. K.: 93
Borsook, Henry: 30
Bowman, Thomas: 339
Brand, Fran Tolley: 665
Brown, Benjamin Chambers: 138, 139
Brown, Owen: 201
Brown, Russell J.: 41
Brownscombe, E. Morley: 163
Bridges: 65, 111, 121, 268
Briggs, Patrick: 316
Buckle, Laurel L.: 290
Buildings: 114, 209, 262, 266, 336, 379, 383, 384, 405, 411, 517, 529, 545, 567, 630, 631 634, 643,
    Central Library (2nd): 51
    Central Library (current): 118, 301, 350
    City Hall: 328, 561
    Pasadena Grand Opera House: 203, 571
    Pasadena Jail: 597, 619, 620
    Royal Laundry Building: 204
Burlingame, Cecil H.: 277
Burton, Tim: 332
Businesses & Economic Conditions: 13, 44, 46, 51, 76, 92, 105, 115, 123, 124, 125; 126, 131, 134, 139, 172, 173, 174, 177, 188, 193, 204, 210, 214, 216, 218, 272, 274, 281, 284, 286, 303, 320, 336, 337, 338, 355, 382, 407, 422, 447, 485, 496, 497, 500, 526, 540, 551, 559, 567, 585, 589, 596, 638, 639, 640, 642, 657, 658, 668, 671
Busch, Lilly: 458, 485

Cairns, Mrs. William Jr.: 245
Carnegie, Andrew, 516
Caswell, Katie: 302
Cattell, Hester F.: 565
Charleville, John W.: 607
Children & Teens: 54, 55, 102, 192, 195, 208, 212, 228, 238, 247, 259, 264, 281, 282, 283, 292, 300, 302, 306, 310, 323, 339, 354, 355, 363, 364, 392, 393, 399, 400, 401, 402, 413, 414, 425, 430, 446, 494, 507, 527, 594, 604, 656, 657, 660, 676
Churches: 229, 234, 299, 320, 454, 458, 504, 505, 507, 559, 631
    All Saints Episcopal: 560
    Church of Scientology: 411
    First Christian: 194
    First Church of the Nazarene: 506, 508, 562
    Lake Avenue Congregational: 215, 239, 445, 446, 448
    Lake Avenue Methodist: 560
    Our Lady of Guadalupe: 536
    Pasadena Jewish Temple: 80
    Pasadena Presbyterian: 627
    Saint Andrew's Church: 71, 253, 541, 542, 543, 544, 545, 546, 547
    Temple B'nai Israel: 35
    West Side Congregational: 397
City of Pasadena; 2, 48, 71, 100, 114, 123, 132, 179, 311, 312, 328, 345, 368, 383, 384, 390, 395, 397, 406, 407, 415, 455, 457, 490, 509, 521, 559, 561, 640
    City Attorney: 498
    City Board of Review: 213, 230, 231, 289, 371, 379, 391
    City Council; 29, 119, 168, 205, 237, 251, 297, 315, 371, 384, 417, 420, 442, 443, 496, 514, 620, 630, 634, 636, 681
    City Manager: 252, 326, 605, 606, 607, 608, 609, 610, 611, 612, 613, 614, 615, 616, 617, 672
    City Planning: 7, 119, 148, 158, 316, 317, 329, 337, 338, 394, 411, 491, 496, 497, 517, 530, 531, 533, 534, 630, 634, 677, 681
    Commission on the Status of Women: 679
    Fire Department: 3, 4, 6, 8, 9, 140, 152, 288, 545
    Health Department: 318
    Human Relations Commission: 506
    Humane Society: 133

Library: 46, 50, 51, 98, 118, 122, 141, 171, 196, 263, 266, 300, 301, 350, 558, 590, 591, 592, 593, 594, 622, 635
    Mayors: 447, 454, 526, 645
    National Guard: 171, 452, 453
    Police Department; 4, 5, 6, 82, 117, 156, 208, 217, 223, 224, 240, 250, 271, 277, 279, 296, 321, 326, 340, 352, 362, 370, 469, 470, 471, 472, 473, 474, 475, 476, 477, 478, 479, 480, 481, 482, 483, 498, 499, 500, 501, 502, 503, 551, 580, 583, 584, 589, 597, 619, 620, 642
    Refuse and Refuse Disposal: 431
    Water and Power: 242, 519, 671
Ching, Albert: 92
Clinton, Hillary Rodham: 257
Clisby, Niel: 308
Clubs & Groups: 97, 177, 226, 278, 353, 356, 357, 458, 515, 623
    American Red Cross: 341, 450, 492
    Americus Club: 649
    Annandale Golf Club: 93, 165, 519
    Cauldron Club: 648
    Boy Scouts: 247, 281, 282
    California Tech Yacht Club: 225
    Girl Scouts: 302, 306, 310, 323, 354, 425
    Ku Klux Klan: 467
    Mexican Settlement House: 677, 678
    Native Sons and Daughters of the Golden West: 237
    Pasadena Audubon Society: 249
    Pasadena Chamber of Commerce: 581
    Pasadena/Foothill Chapter of the ACLU: 668
    Pasadena Heritage: 65
    Pasadena Hospitality House: 637
    Pasadena Patriots: 69
    Pasadena Playhouse: 210, 440, 525, 537, 539, 540, 548, 572, 675
    Shakespeare Club: 509
    Valley Hunt Club: 143, 166
    Women's Christian Temperance Union: 441, 442, 443, 444
Colby, Lillie A.: 270
Coleman, Isabella: 172
Congressional Medal of Honor SEE Medal of Honor
Connelly, W. H.: 68

Cooper-Harris, Tracey: 588
Corcoran, Tea: 430
Coulombe, Joe: 216
Courage, New Hampshire: 188
Cowie, Bessie Lee: 285
Crime & Criminals: 50, 82, 100; 142, 156, 240, 340, 362, 415, 420, 470, 471, 472, 476, 477, 478, 479, 480, 482, 489, 493, 496, 497, 498, 501, 503, 504, 506, 509, 580, 597, 619, 620, 672
    9/11: 37
    Animal welfare: 133
    Alcohol related: 68, 551
    Arson: 137
    Burglary: 191, 277, 296, 332, 377, 378, 410, 618
    Demonstrations: 117, 208, 321
    Extortion: 93, 642
    Gambling: 250, 481
    Kidnapping: 339
    Misuse of 911: 223, 224
    Murder: 34, 36, 75, 76, 250, 343, 586
    Not being registered: 246, 495
    Parking: 237
Crown City Rockers (Musical group): 45
Culver, Lee R.: 472
Curtis, Richard: 283

Death & Health: 3, 8, 9, 25, 26, 27, 56, 72, 104, 106, 111, 112, 113; 121, 127, 131, 133, 136, 150, 153, 156, 161, 162, 163, 165, 169, 185, 189, 199, 205, 212, 250, 267, 270, 273, 291, 305, 309, 314, 318, 322, 327, 358, 373, 374, 375, 383, 384, 438, 452, 453, 487, 488, 492, 505, 591, 592, 593, 644, 651
Devil's Gate Dam: 211
Dewitt, Evelyn Lindy: 181
Dill, Myrle A.: 137
Dickinson, Emma E.: 521
Disasters & Accidents: 3, 4, 8, 12, 14, 26, 56, 131, 136, 140, 151, 152, 154, 162, 163, 164, 169, 178, 187, 192, 199, 212, 236, 270, 303, 327, 358, 373, 374, 375, 398, 408, 466, 523, 536, 579, 674, 680
Dowling, Frank J.: 194
Draper, Erwin C.: 3

Dunn, Mrs. J. C.
Dunbar, Diane: 16
Dunn-Webb, Gurlay: 90

Eaton, Wendell: 288
Elections: 33, 60, 197, 237, 257, 278, 417, 420, 519, 667, 681
England, John C.: 109
Ethnic Communities: 101,107, 234, 246, 307, 429, 494, 495, 504, 506,527, 541, 549, 551, 598, 668
    African American: 7, 56, 110, 175, 179, 213, 219, 220, 262, 299, 308, 417, 432, 433, 451, 514, 595, 629, 650, 655
    Chinese American: 61, 64, 92, 199
    German Americans: 618, 622
    Hispanic Americans: 75, 255, 271, 273, 314, 342, 343, 487, 536, 546, 550, 597, 658, 659, 675, 676, 677, 678
    Iranian American: 70
    Japanese American: 106, 259, 303, 304, 418, 463
    Jewish American: 35, 80, 88
    Korean Americans; 99
    Native Americans: 283

Fanous, Mike: 300
Ferguson, Sarah: 468
Finney, F. N.: 394
Forrest, Mollie: 233
Fox, Charles J.: 524
Franklin, Thomas: 29
Freeman, Robert: 396
French, William J.: 149
Fronimos, James E.: 580

Gavel-Briggs, Mary: 316
Garcia, Richard Edward: 487
Geography: 63, 125, 283, 287, 288, 330, 343, 479, 485, 491, 507, 516, 519, 526, 579, 585, 586, 602, 644, 646
    Arroyo Seco: 19, 111, 121, 159, 160, 211, 241, 243, 521, 531, 532, 533, 534, 535
    Chihuahita: 255
    Eaton Canyon: 583, 584, 680,

Linda Vista: 268, 513, 534,
Pasadena Center; 120, 227
Pasadena Civic Auditorium: 117, 144, 670
Plaza Pasadena Mall: 673
San Gabriel Mountains: 147, 164, 270, 502
Streets; 43, 237
    Arroyo Parkway: 280, 580
    California Boulevard: 677
    Colorado Boulevard: 119, 146, 209, 251, 262, 311, 312, 338, 490, 528, 530
    Lake Avenue, 335, 337, 596
    Raymond Avenue: 203, 204, 219
    Woodlyn Road: 317
Gillette, Cindy: 413,
Glass, Montague: 240
Glass, Wesley: 629
Gobrecht, Chris: 684
Goff, Dorothy Gill: 408
Goodall, Oliver: 262
Gorby, Melba: 666
Grimes, Charles: 126
Gudiel, Rose: 274
Gunter, Elder: 611

Hagen, Walter: 97
Halbe, William Lewis: 250
Hamlisch, Marvin: 145
Hammer, Anna: 82
Han, Sam: 99
Haney, Oliver: 113
Harding, Warren G.: 55
Hartwell, Calvin: 447
Hawkey, Philip: 614
Hawkins, Gordon: 56
Hay, Helen: 564
Herms, George: 191
Hernandez, Ruben: 229
Hibbard, William Edwards: 169
Hines, Harold: 608

Hines, La Vieve M.: 601
Hines, Richard R., Jr.: 17
Hitchcock, L. Potter: 397
Hitchcock, Madeline: 153
Hobbs, Katherine: 566
Holder, Charles Frederick: 184
Holidays
    Admission Day: 171
    Chinese New Year: 61, 64
    Christmas: 116, 186, 222, 338
    Cinco de Mayo: 659
    Fourth of July: 83, 444, 570
    Iranian New Year: 70
    New Year's: 275
Holt, Ben: 671
Hoocker, Louise R.: 420
Hoover, Herbert: 197, 664
Hotels: 493
    Constance: 148
    Green: 523
    Huntington: 178, 522, 529, 538
    Maryland: 601, 645
    Raymond: 221, 595
    Vista del Arroyo: 460
Hoxsey, Archibald: 374
Humphries, Carrie: 427
Humble, Melvill: 121
Hunt, Jane: 635
Huntington, Howard: 517
Hurd, Gale Anne: 76

Interesting Pasadenans; 3, 4, 5, 9, 16, 17, 19, 20, 26, 29, 30, 34, 36, 37, 40, 41, 56, 59, 62, 68, 75, 76, 79, 82, 84, 85, 86, 90, 91, 92, 93, 95, 99, 108, 109, 110, 111, 113, 116, 121, 124, 126, 135; 136, 137, 138, 139, 142, 145, 149; 150; 153, 157, 161, 163, 165, 166, 167, 168, 169, 170, 172, 175, 177, 179, 181, 184, 185, 189, 191, 194, 200, 201, 202, 212, 216, 228, 229, 233, 235, 236, 240, 242, 244, 245, 250, 252, 253, 254, 258, 259, 260, 262, 264, 267, 270, 271, 273, 274, 277, 283, 285, 288, 290, 291, 296, 299, 300, 301, 302, 303, 304, 305, 308, 313,

314, 316, 317, 319, 322, 323, 325, 326, 327, 332, 334, 339, 340, 342, 343, 344, 349, 351, 352, 353, 354, 359, 360, 365, 366, 367, 368, 370, 372, 373, 374, 381, 389, 394, 397, 408, 409, 410, 413, 414, 417, 420, 427, 430, 432, 433, 440, 447, 449, 454, 455, 458, 459, 460, 461, 462, 463, 464, 465, 469, 472, 473, 474, 475, 476, 477, 481, 483, 484, 485, 486, 487, 488, 489, 502, 506, 508, 510, 511, 514, 517, 520, 521, 524, 526, 535, 538, 542, 555, 562, 564, 565, 566, 569, 573, 574, 578, 580, 581, 582, 588, 595, 601, 602, 603, 605, 606, 607, 608, 609, 610, 611, 612, 613, 614, 615, 616, 617, 627, 629, 633, 635, 636, 638, 641, 642, 647, 650, 651, 655, 658, 665, 666, 669, 676, 681, 684

Jackson, Michael: 297, 298, 299
Jacobs, William; 26
Jacobson, J.: 236
Jet Propulsion Laboratory: 187, 377, 378
Johnson, Charles: 110
Johnson, Hiram: 49
Johnson, John: 62
Johnston, Helen Berry: 469
Judy, Ann Clary: 352

Kathleen's on Lake: 596
Kaufmann, Gordon: 459
Kerry, John: 324
Kersten, Harry R.: 340
Koiner, C. Wellington: 242, 326, 605
Klotzle, John: 16
Kral, Thomas: 260
Kuranaga, Frank T.: 303, 304
Kurtz, Cynthia: 615

Lang, Robert: 20
Lawrence, J. C.: 481
Lee, Wilson J.: 651
Logan, James, 595
Lormer, Florence: 200
Lopez, Eva: 676
Ludlow, Fred: 370

MacKenzie, Douglas C.: 368
MacLean, Elizabeth: 161
Maravich, Pete: 505
McCarthy, John M.: 253
McClanahan, Officer: 4, 5
McCurdy, Robert M.: 609
McHale, Jim: 520
McIntyre, Don: 613,
McMillan, Don C.: 252, 610
Medal of Honor: 460, 461, 462
Media
    Movies: 63, 213, 230, 231, 235, 289, 371, 376, 408, 578, 670
    Newspapers: 198
    Radio: 15, 439, 445, 623, 624, 625, 626, 627
    Television: 76, 190, 202, 287, 288, 440
Melekian, Bernard: 616
Merritt, Huelett Clinton: 489
Miller, Ruth: 157
Millikan, Robert: 644
Modjeska, Helena: 571
Mora, Francisco Javier: 75
Morris, Clarence H.: 291

Nash, John: 67
Nehdar, Nat: 506
Noor, Queen of Jordan: 73

Obama, Michelle: 183
Orbison, Robert Vance: 606
Outten, Edgar C.: 457
O'Rourke, Robert Emmett: 476, 477

Paddock, Charles W.: 167, 235, 244
Page, Jay: 121
Paige, David Abbey: 465
Paparian, William: 636
Parks: 107, 507, 521
    Brookside: 515, 531, 532, 533, 535, 575,
    Carmelita: 390, 394, 395, 399, 400, 435

      Central: 387, 421, 652
      Memorial: 182, 256
      Tournament: 130, 294, 385, 386, 396
Parks, J. S.: 168
Pasadena Museum of Art: 191
Parsons Corporation: 218
Patterson, John Neil: 334
Patton-Badder, Patti: 313
Peace through Music: 506
Peterson, Linda: 212
Phillips, John D.: 612
Pierce, Grace Adele: 349
Puckett, John: 359
Pursell, Marion Weimer: 296

Ramirez, Rogelio: 314
Ray, Sugar: 66
Reagan, James W.: 535
Reed, Albert Clark: 360
Reed, Tom, 126
Reynolds, J. O.: 502
Reynolds, Kenyon L.: 542
Reynolds, Raul T.: 655
Rhodes, Jeremiah M.: 582
Richard, Isaac: 514
Riddle, Phlunte: 179
Robinson, Jackie: 86, 175, 432, 433
Robledo, Canuto: 273
Rockefeller, John D.: 585, 587
Rogers, Paul: 116
Romero, Raul: 75
Roosevelt, Theodore: 375
Rose Bowl: 4, 6, 66, 83, 158, 297, 329, 331, 403, 439, 533, 534, 535, 570, 599, 600, 661, 663
Rustin, Manuel: 59

Sanchez, Philip J.: 271
Scherer, James A. B.: 366
Schiff, Adam: 508

Schmitt, Harrison H.: 344
Schools: 36, 54, 55, 102, 269, 314, 439, 527, 582, 604, 650, 656, 657, 658, 668
    California Institute of Technology: 10, 15, 20, 25, 26, 27, 28, 29, 30, 31, 32, 62, 75, 81, 95, 105, 128, 135, 189, 225, 268, 327, 333, 344, 346, 356, 357, 360, 366, 367, 369, 376, 511, 512, 552, 644 SEE ALSO Throop Polytechnic Institute
    Columbia Grammar: 392, 393
    Fuller Theological Seminary: 682
    Grover Cleveland Elementary: 307
    James A. Garfield Elementary: 53
    James Madison Elementary School: 392
    John Muir High: 59, 325, 510
    Mayfield: 248, 282, 306, 363, 389
    New Horizon School: 101, 364
    Pasadena City College: 57, 58, 106, 109, 206, 207, 208, 267, 284, 324, 683, 684
    Pasadena Junior College SEE Pasadena City College
    Pasadena High: 147, 192, 195, 380, 662
    Pasadena Part-time: 660
    Pasadena Poly: 258
    Saint Andrew's: 544
    Sequoyah: 364, 388, 401
    Throop Polytechnic Institute: 23, 24, 128, 549 SEE ALSO California Institute of Technology
    Walden School: 402
    William McKinley School: 393
Scott, Betty: 267
Selementi, M. A.: 93
Simms, Ron: 427
Singleton, Mildred: 170
Sirhan, Sirhan Bishara: 36
Slavin, Matthew: 177
Smith, Erwin: 165
Smith, Lucious W.: 299
Smith, Robert Weston: 538
Socialists: 166
Spangler, James E.: 650
Sports: 140, 159, 160, 176, 178, 206, 207, 221, 228, 261, 275, 279,

300, 386, 399, 400, 403, 419, 432, 473, 474, 521, 531, 553, 556, 560, 599, 601, 643, 652, 683, 684
    Baseball: 86, 91, 130, 173, 175, 238, 293, 294, 295, 350, 428, 429, 433, 435, 440, 549, 550
    Basketball: 505
    Boxing: 243, 273,
    Firearms: 583, 584
    Football: 4, 6, 56, 128, 155, 158, 329, 330, 331, 380, 423, 439, 533, 534, 600
    Golf: 81, 97, 252, 515, 519, 532, 575, 586, 595
    Olympics & Olympians: 103, 157, 167, 170, 235, 510, 524
    Polo: 385, 396
    Soccer: 552, 554, 555, 689
    Track and Field: 167, 170, 235, 244, 510
    Tennis: 573
    Volleyball: 389
Spurlock, Lynn: 414
Steele, Isobel Lillian: 416

Taft, William Howard: 632
Talbot, Ida May: 9
Tatum, Larry: 228
Taylor, Edward J.: 449
Technology: 1, 11, 12, 14, 15, 23, 24, 27, 28, 62, 95, 151, 164, 187, 189, 201, 217, 224, 237, 242, 351, 372, 373, 374, 375, 377, 381, 424, 471, 480, 518, 621, 644, 656, 660, 671, 674
Telles, Martin: 343
Thayer, Floyd Gerald: 108
Thelen, Jennifer: 389
Thou Shall Not: 100, 113, 338, 345, 362, 369, 397, 406, 414, 442, 444, 482, 497, 501, 629, 677, 682
    Do offensive things to your property: 316
    Drink alcohol: 278, 285, 551, 561
    Make Noise: 251, 297, 426, 584
    Offend Public Morality: 191, 213, 230, 231, 233, 238, 289, 307, 371, 379, 391, 397, 443, 479, 481, 622
    Park Illegally: 119
    Smoke: 112, 131, 441
    Use the Rose Bowl: 158, 297, 534

Toltschin, R. D.: 455
Tournament of Roses: 154, 275, 424, 426, 431, 434, 553
    Floats: 85, 172, 202, 412, 427
    Football Game: 155, 331, 423
    Horses: 174
    Grand Marshal: 89, 365, 685, 686, 687, 688
    Queen and Princesses: 292, 413, 414, 425, 430, 510, 573, 574, 576, 578
Townsend, Julie: 323
Trader Joe's: 216
Transportation: 370, 386, 491, 580, 621, 660, 665
    Airplanes: 151, 372, 373, 374, 375, 455, 480, 579, 641, 656, 666
    Automobiles: 1, 10, 11, 12, 14, 192, 237, 242, 470
    Buses: 527, 604
    Helicopters: 248, 426
    Motorcycles: 503
    Ships: 328, 486
    Trains: 94, 201, 444
    UFOs: 31, 32
Tuffy, Lucky: 84

Upshaw, Garrie M.: 473, 474
Ustick, Richard: 40

Vertical Wine Bistro: 76
Visitors: 47, 48, 123, 147, 148, 183, 215, 347, 404, 516, 523, 543, 585, 587, 653
    Nobel Prize Winners: 21, 22
    Entertainers: 66, 146, 182, 202, 234, 297, 298, 348, 522, 571, 661, 662, 663, 670
    Politicians: 33, 49, 52, 60, 197, 257, 324, 525, 667
    Presidents: 54, 55, 375, 628, 632, 645, 664, 685, 686, 687, 688, 689
    Royalty: 73, 309, 434, 468, 563
    Smart People: 67, 89, 96
    Sports People: 97, 130, 243, 293, 294, 295, 435, 505, 553, 575, 652

Walton, Maurice: 522
War: 18, 333, 450, 460, 655
    Spanish-American War: 108, 449, 451, 633, 651
    Punitive Expedition into Mexico: 452, 453
    World War One: 23, 24, 104, 138, 149, 220, 281, 286, 436, 437, 438, 485, 486, 489, 494, 495, 618, 622, 654
    World War Two: 29, 38, 109, 148, 161, 200, 205, 232, 258, 259, 267, 291, 309, 326, 328, 359, 381, 418, 440, 455, 456, 459, 462, 463, 464, 486, 487, 488, 583, 597, 626, 629, 630, 634, 637, 638, 639, 640
    Korean War: 2, 16, 17, 40, 41, 269, 462
    Philippine-American War: 461
    Vietnamese War: 78, 106, 150, 185, 222, 290, 319, 354
    9/11: 37, 39, 42, 43
    Iraq: 218, 313, 314, 315, 320, 321, 322, 325
Warren, Jack: 511
Waterhouse, William: 454
White Hut Restaurant: 92
White, Margaret: 111
Whitley, Dion: 325
Williams, Dick: 91
Winders, Timothy W.: 354
Worcester, Anthony: 488
Wostry, Carlo: 543
Woodbury, Joan: 574
Women: 9, 13, 16, 72, 76, 82, 85, 90, 111, 136, 137, 141, 142, 153, 157, 161, 170, 172, 179, 181, 198, 200, 212, 222, 224, 233, 245, 264, 267, 270, 284, 285, 286, 290, 292, 301, 302, 304, 306, 310, 313, 323, 342, 349, 351, 352, 353, 354, 355, 363, 389, 408, 409, 410, 413, 414, 415, 420, 422, 425, 430, 441, 442, 443, 444, 458, 478, 484, 494, 495, 499, 509, 512, 521, 564, 565, 566, 569, 573, 574, 576, 578, 588, 601, 635, 637, 658, 665, 666, 676, 679, 683, 684
Wright, Mrs. W. S.: 410
Wright, Tonika Stayduhar: 409

Yokaitis: Don: 681
Yomagashi, Ko: 259

Zimmerman, David Paul: 185

**1800's:** 128, 147, 171, 184, 199, 209, 348, 429, 447, 449, 451, 518, 621, 633, 651
**1900's**: 46, 64, 130, 133, 176, 177, 194, 233, 245, 246, 275, 276, 303, 304, 393, 396, 399, 423, 444, 446, 454, 517, 545, 550, 551, 561, 574, 576, 585, 586, 587, 595, 632, 635
**1910's:** 21, 22, 47, 48, 49, 50, 51, 61, 90, 122, 123, 125, 126, 138, 141, 154, 155, 169, 173, 196, 198, 213, 219, 220, 236, 238, 242, 249, 253, 263, 281, 286, 293, 294, 295, 345, 349, 355, 362, 385, 386, 387, 392, 394, 395, 397, 400, 415, 428, 436, 437, 438, 452, 453, 458, 485, 492, 493, 494, 495, 496, 498, 500, 501, 502, 504, 516, 519, 522, 523, 529, 541, 549, 553, 558, 560, 563, 577, 591, 592, 593, 594, 618, 622, 647, 648, 649, 654, 657, 662, 669
**1920's**: 5, 7, 53, 56, 57, 58, 68, 81, 97, 103, 121, 127, 128, 134, 142, 159, 163, 167, 168, 178, 193, 195, 203, 221, 230, 231, 234, 235, 240, 250, 264, 268, 270, 278, 279, 280, 296, 307, 308, 318, 341, 342, 343, 353, 366, 371, 379, 410, 417, 420, 435, 436, 437, 438, 439, 442, 443, 470, 472, 475, 477, 478, 479, 481, 482, 483, 485, 499, 521, 531, 532, 535, 548, 605, 606, 624, 645, 653, 658, 665, 675
**1930's:** 4, 8, 83, 111, 131, 132, 136, 137, 149, 162, 164, 206, 207, 210, 243, 251, 289, 327, 329, 347, 365, 369, 370, 404, 416, 419, 420, 465, 474, 512, 520, 521, 524, 525, 528, 530, 552, 599, 600, 601, 605, 606, 607, 627, 631, 641, 642, 643, 644, 652, 664, 666, 676, 677, 678
**1940's**: 3, 26, 30, 38, 82,140, 148, 152, 153, 156, 158, 161, 200, 205, 211, 232, 237, 258, 259, 261, 267, 284, 285, 291, 305, 309, 326, 328, 330, 335, 340, 346, 359, 381, 383, 384, 407, 418, 431, 432, 455, 456, 457, 459, 462, 463, 464, 486, 487, 488, 509, 511, 513, 575, 580, 583, 597, 605, 608, 609, 610, 623, 626, 629, 630, 634, 636, 637, 638, 639, 640
**1950's:** 2, 31, 72, 86, 170, 212, 252, 317, 328, 337, 339, 388, 390, 398, 430, 433, 462, 466, 490, 491, 537, 542, 581, 610
**1960's**: 32, 33, 34, 78, 143, 174, 185, 191, 222, 269, 290, 319, 338, 354, 381, 382, 391, 405, 413, 445, 559, 610, 611, 612
**1970's:** 106, 115, 292, 344, 422, 497, 497, 527, 562, 598, 604, 612, 613, 625, 650, 667, 668, 670, 671, 672, 673, 679, 680, 681, 682, 683
**1980's:** 71, 88, 102, 223, 224, 297, 427, 505, 515, 538, 539, 562, 566, 613, 620,
**1990's:** 75, 101, 215, 356, 389, 406, 414, 468, 547, 572, 613, 614, 615, 619, 636

**2000's:** 37, 39, 42, 43, 73, 89, 91, 101, 117, 120, 204, 218, 248, 257, 282, 299, 302, 306, 310, 313, 314, 315, 316, 320, 321, 322, 324, 325, 332, 351, 352, 357, 358, 359, 363, 402, 403, 507, 556, 557, 570, 584, 615, 616, 617, 646, 663

**2010's:** 52, 59, 60, 62, 66, 67, 70, 77, 79, 87, 94, 95, 96, 100, 107, 120, 160, 180, 187, 226, 256, 262, 271, 272, 274, 288, 323, 411, 540, 588, 617, 661, 674

**About the author:**

Dan McLaughlin was born in Hollywood during halftime of a Rams-Colts game. Although the Rams scored a touchdown soon after his birth to tie the game, the Colts then scored 17 points to win. This, along with multi-decade stints at UCLA and as a government bureaucrat, has given Dan an appreciation for the subtle and sometimes capricious agency of action and words.

Among his philosophical influences he cites Thomas Kuhn, David Springhorn, Paul Feyerabend, the Reduced Shakespeare Company and Bullwinkle the Moose. When not working as the local history reference librarian at the Pasadena Public Library, Dan can be found working merrily in the garden, pacing nervously during any UCLA game where the lead is less than 25 points, or walking sedately the beloved puppies with his even more beloved honey, Vendi.

Dan has written five novels, two non-fiction works on the history of Pasadena, one musical and a play. In reverse chronological order his works of fiction have been: "WereKitty" a work which considers what happens 20 years after a torrid love affair between a normal human and a member of the differentially animated community; "Gott Mit Uns" a play that tells the story of an 8 1/2 foot penguin, who is a goddess, who is pursued by two people, who are bureaucrats, through today's America; "Mime Time" a murder mystery about a mime about to be nominated the Republican presidential candidate of 2012 and the people who want to kill him; "Gott Mit Uns" the novel which is the source of his recent play; "Pass the Damn Salt, Please" a novel which explores the importance of language and politeness in relationships told entirely in dialogue; "ICE Girls" an award winning novella which examines the story of the Little Match Girl from the point of view of management; "Oh No, Not Emily!" an operetta in which a modern fake Emily Dickinson poem is sold to a post-modern English Department.

Two of Dan's works have been nominated for Just Plain Folks awards: "Oh No, Not Emily!" for Best Theater Album, and "ICE Girls" for Best Storytelling Album.

With Mark Sellin and other friends, Dan wrote, directed and acted in several plays at the Renaissance Faire in Southern California, including their greatest hit "Ye Olde Tale of Goode King Arthur." He also has created radio play versions of the Trojan Horse "The Big Horsey Ride" and the Odyssey "Going Home and Getting Lucky."

Along with Mark, Dan was part of the folk/comedy phenomenon "2 Guys from the 70's" mostly in the 1980's.

In terms of his non-fiction, Dan has been the local history librarian at the Pasadena Public Library for over 25 years. He has answered reference questions and provided individualized instruction for hundreds of library patrons over the years. He has also designed and contributed content to two local history databases: the Pasadena Digital History Collaborative and the Pasadena News Index. "Pasadena History Headline Quiz" is the first part of a projected trilogy on the history of Pasadena for grade schoolers. Questions from this book are also sprinkled liberally through his other Pasadena history book, "Pasadena: A Mystery and a History You Can Explore." As far as he can figure out now, the third part will be a book on the historical geography of Pasadena.

Made in United States
Troutdale, OR
12/17/2023

15958393R00135